EARTHLY AND COSMIC MAN

Rudolf Steiner

EARTHLY AND COSMIC MAN

Nine lectures held in Berlin on October 23, 1911, and between March 19 and June 20, 1912

TRANSLATION BY
DOROTHY OSMOND AND CLIFFORD VENHO

RUDOLF STEINER

SteinerBooks

CW 133

SteinerBooks | Anthroposophic Press
834 Main Street, P.O. Box 358
Spencertown, New York 12165
www.steinerbooks.org

Original translation from German by Dorothy Osmond and Clifford Venho
Introduction by Marie Steiner

This book is volume 133 in the Collected Works (CW) of Rudolf Steiner, published by SteinerBooks, 2025. It is a translation of *Der irdische und der kosmische Mensch*, 4th edition, published by Rudolf Steiner Verlag, Dornach, Switzerland, 1989.

ISBN: 978-1-62148-384-7
eBook ISBN: 978-1-62148-385-4

Printed in the United States of America
by Integrated Books International

CONTENTS

INTRODUCTION

THE WEALTH OF ideas and spiritual treasures bestowed upon us by Rudolf Steiner in his lectures often makes it difficult to arrange certain series of lectures under one category and heading. They are like concentrated points of energy from which sparks shoot out in every direction, lighting up the near and the far, piercing their way to the primal beginnings and again into infinitudes of space and time—then giving sharp definition to details which may seem unessential but are of great symptomatic importance. Out of the cumulative mass of details, the necessities of storm-charged destiny arise but also a sustaining power of the spirit. We discern the play of forces which preceded the sufferings of our present time, discharged itself with unparalleled fury in the World War and its aftermath and will burst out in tempests yet to come. We understand why this had to be, what failings will be forgiven, what demands made of us. A great and impressive tableau of history unrolls from the precision given to details otherwise ignored and from the vast cosmic-human background against which the life of man stands out in bold relief.

These vistas of primordial cosmic happenings, of ages of gray antiquity in human history which, nevertheless, shed clearest light upon our present time, are opened up with particular vividness in the lectures given to members of the Anthroposophical Society—with certain interruptions, but in constantly recurring rhythm—in places where Rudolf Steiner made his home between continual travelling: Berlin and Dornach. The lectures were given in order that the conscience of a small group of human beings at least might be made alive to the tasks of the time, to the vital significance of the hour in which we were living before the World War, and are still living today.

Rudolf Steiner spoke gravely and impressively, like the voice of destiny itself, like the awakened human conscience, linking his arguments with factual details in every sphere. And then, when in the world outside, all supports hitherto thought secure, tottered for every eye to see, as the forces burst upon one another with elemental might, it was he who tried ever and again to formulate the thoughts of deliverance and recovery without which chaos cannot be overcome. Although an unfledged humanity could not understand this voice, a light must somehow be brought into the chaos—even though it might reach only a small group of immature but eager-hearted people. An attempt had also to be made to penetrate here and there into the field of concrete, practical life. To be sure, the representatives of this "practical side of life," as they are pleased to call it, scornfully and with vicious measures of sabotage, rejected everything that seemed to them so remote from reality in that it spoke of spiritual worlds. Yet the living thought has the power to outlast the moment and to rise up again in a new form. Its duty is to work even where there is no prospect of success; in all its purity it has to find its way to souls who, through constant testing, gradually become open to receive it. Out of the concrete realities of existence from which his spiritual vision was never willing to withdraw, Rudolf Steiner created a science of knowledge embracing every domain of life and able to pour vitalizing, creative impulses into the manifold branches of science and art, philosophy and religious activity.

To live through this was, and remains, an intense upliftment, like climbing up steep mountain crests in snow-cleansed, sun-pierced air. Deep, refreshing breaths can be drawn in this region of the higher cosmic realities which imbue human life with meaning and even now shape the picture of destiny in those future times, when, out of a quickened consciousness, thought will encompass higher and higher spheres of existence.

Treasures of the spirit of well-nigh frightening brilliance have been bequeathed to us, demonstrating through their very existence that the might of the Dark Age, of Kali Yuga, has been broken and conquered. True, the darkness is within us still, but the light is there and may not be withheld—not even from a humanity living in shadow.

The light—of which Rudolf Steiner says that it is the Christ-impulse—had first to prepare and shape the vessel of human consciousness into which it can flow; it will bring to human beings that re-awakening by which alone they can wrest themselves from downfall.

Neither the powers of the sentient soul nor the fervent passion of religious experience known to the Middle Ages, to the saints and the mystics along the path of the Christian initiation, are competent to overcome the obstructions brought by the age of rationalism. But wise providence, guide and leader of human existence, inaugurated, even before the dawn of the modern age, a second path of Christian initiation along which souls were gradually to be made ready for the demands of a later future.

The call of this, the Christian-Rosicrucian path, went out above all to the powers of the consciousness soul. Hence its mission was also to establish the human being firmly within the personality, to allow him to experience to the full the significance of the single life. Through study, through imagination and contemplation, it led the human being out into the macrocosm—which was discovered again, in image, within his own being. But the full development of the forces of the personality, whereby the I could be led to conscious realization of the spirit, made it necessary that the knowledge of repeated earth-lives should, to begin with, be hidden for a time from the portion of humanity destined to unfold these forces of personality.

What the new age needs is not a return to the past through a revival of the methods of yoga, nor of the Gnostic or Rosicrucian paths in the form in which they served the spiritual good of humanity in days gone by. In accordance with the demands of the modern age, a new impulse must be given to the rigorous path of Rosicrucian knowledge, which in its true form has nothing whatever to do with the charlatanry that has usurped its name—a new impulse, in the form of the revelation of the great truths of reincarnation and karma.

Until the task of proclaiming these truths devolved upon Rudolf Steiner, Rosicrucianism concealed them, kept silence about them. But it came about that with the passage of the centuries, these truths were able to flash into the consciousness of minds in Europe, as the result of rigorous and strenuous ways of thought, and as a fruit of knowledge born of alert reason; as a concern, too, of mankind, through which the evolution of human history receives meaning and significance, not as a concern of the single individual whose goal, as in Buddhism, is liberation from the wheel of rebirth. We need only mention the names of Goethe and Lessing.

The salvation of the individuality passing onwards and unfolding through the recurrent earthly lives, the rebirth of the divine I in man—this is the deed wrought by Christ, and with the stupendous power of knowledge at his command Rudolf Steiner brought this deed ever and again before our eyes.

When after long reluctance he had made up his mind to comply with the request of German theosophists to lead their work, he was able to accept the proposal because of the avowed task of the Theosophical Society: to establish knowledge of reincarnation and karma in the world. The lectures leading to the request that he should become the leader of this movement in Germany were those on *Mysticism at the Dawn of Modern Spiritual Life*, and *Christianity as Mystical Fact*. Therewith, the impulse which he was to bring to the movement had been clearly indicated, and he was assured of absolute freedom to teach as he would. He himself acted in line with the spirit of true occultists of all ages who make a link with the store of spiritual knowledge already existing in order to preserve its life and lead it forward. He still saw hope of being able, through the new impulse, to rescue the Theosophical Society, too, from lapsing into the rigidity of dogma, to imbue it with fresh forces and enrich its very defective understanding of the mysteries of Christianity.

Without overthrowing anything at all, gradually laying stone upon stone, he created the basis for this understanding. For the new insight must be acquired by the listeners only through knowledge consciously put to the test of reason. And so, to begin with, he adopted the terminology current among the theosophists, gradually widening the ideas and giving them life so that they might conform to the more alert consciousness of the modern mind. The basis once created, wider and wider perspectives could be opened out, until, from the side of the suprasensory, there broke the light which reveals the mission of the earth and the tasks of mankind.

Not only from the point of view of their content, but also from that of chronology, the opportunity of studying every such series of lectures given by Rudolf Steiner seems to us to be of great importance for newcomers to spiritual science, for only so is it possible to realize the living, organic growth of the work. Remarks interpolated here and there in the lectures about contemporary happenings seeming to have little bearing at a later time, have such moral and educational value that they are of lasting significance.

There can be no concealment of the firm stand Rudolf Steiner was compelled to take against the attempts that were clouding objective truth and corrupting the Theosophical Society by the introduction of pet projects and personal ambitions. The warnings given in this connection may not always be understood by the reader today. In the main, they were connected with the occult despotism—for so indeed it may be called—which took the form of the announcement of the coming of a World Savior in the flesh—to whom they dared to give the name of Christ. The Indian boy Krishnamurti was chosen for this role and the "Order of the Star in the East" founded with a flourish of trumpets. The Theosophical Society was expected to place itself in the service of this new aim. By these crude means it was hoped to win souls who were open to listen to the explanations of Christian esotericism given by Rudolf Steiner. But a campaign, fought with all the arms of calumny, was launched against him. The International Theosophical Congress which was to have been held in Genoa in the year 1911 and in which Rudolf Steiner was to have given two lectures on "Buddhism in the twentieth century" and "Christ in the twentieth century," was cancelled at the last minute for inadequate reasons—but in reality because of fear that the influence of Dr. Steiner's words might be too strong. In the lectures that year, many references had to be made to this affair, which for very many people was absolutely incomprehensible.

It had become necessary to make it clear that methods so grievously degrading the level of the Theosophical Society could not be countenanced. Dr. Steiner stated this firmly, but with pain, and pouring his very heart's blood into the words, he spoke repeatedly of his one great wish—that the Society led by him might not succumb to the failings into which occult societies so easily lapse when they fall short of the demands of strict truthfulness and drift into vanity and ambition.

The words should live like cleansing flames in the souls of those who represent his work and over and over again arise before them as an exhortation and warning.

The lectures given in Berlin in the year 1912 contain many references to the struggles Rudolf Steiner was obliged to face in order that, in spite of hidden attacks, the spirit of such a movement might be rescued in its purity, for spiritual science. The lapse in the Theosophical Society made it necessary to lay sharp emphasis upon the autonomy of the anthroposophical work in Middle Europe *vis-à-vis* the Anglo-Indian Theosophical Society, and during the last days of December 1912, the "Anthroposophical League [*Bund*]" was officially founded. The rhythms of the years recall such days vividly to the memory.

Thirty years ago, on October 20, 1902, in Berlin, Rudolf Steiner gave his first lecture on anthroposophy, and on October 21 translated into German the theosophical lecture delivered by Annie Besant who at that time had not come under the sway of the unhealthy influences to which she afterwards fell victim. Twenty years ago, Rudolf Steiner was obliged to protect the anthroposophical movement inaugurated by him from the despotic attacks going out from Adyar, and to speak the words which are like a heritage left by the lectures and are now being made available to us once again as a memorial of those days. They rang out in power during the last days of December of that same year, in Cologne, when in Rudolf Steiner's lectures on *The Bhagavad Gita and the Epistles of St. Paul* the purest oriental wisdom was presented to the listeners with unprecedented grandeur, in the light of Christian knowledge.

Again his concluding words were an impressive appeal for self-knowledge and humility in those belonging to the movement inaugurated by him. But the opposing powers were not slumbering. Ten years ago, on New Year's Eve, 1922/23, the Goetheanum was in flames. Only the Group, sculptured in wood, portraying the Representative of Humanity between the vanquished Adversaries, was saved. We are hoping that by Christmas of this year, this Group will stand in a space worthy of it, in the new Goetheanum. There is a moving description of the Representative of Humanity, of the Christ Figure, at the end of one of the lectures of 1912, when there was no thought—even of the possibility—of its execution in sculpture. It came before us then in words, and now it stands before our eyes as a work of art.

Marie Steiner
December 1932

EARTHLY AND COSMIC MAN

Rudolf Steiner

Lecture One

BERLIN, OCTOBER 23, 1911

Now that we are together again after a rather lengthy summer interval, a few words may be said about what has been happening in our movement meanwhile, particularly about activities which have by no means been without significance for our work in Middle Europe. You know that from the time we were last together here before the summer interval, preparations were in train for the meeting at Munich,[†] which generally begins with a dramatic performance produced in a form appropriate to the spirit of our movement. During the last few years, we have been able to develop this dramatic work. We began, first of all, by having one such performance before a course of lectures in Munich, last year we were able to give two performances, and this year we have been able to attempt three. These performances are always, of course, a somewhat hazardous enterprise, but thanks to the ready self-sacrifice of those who helped with their production, we really have succeeded in making a beginning—the beginning of something which, as it develops, will be a very important impulse in anthroposophical life when we ourselves shall no longer be able to be present in the physical body. But things of this kind—which extend far beyond the narrow limits of personal activity—must have a beginning somewhere, and those who participate in them must realize—in order that they may have the due humility and strength—that they are nothing more than a beginning. These performances, combined as they always are with a course of lectures, bring together not only members of our own section but also many friends of the movement who now come to Munich from all over Europe. Those who try to understand the outer and the inner aspects of these activities may have been particularly struck this year by two things. The first is the way in which we are striving to carry the impulse of anthroposophy, to begin with, into art. Our aim, of course, is that the spiritual life will be carried into every branch and sphere of existence. The reason why it seems so important to bring this spiritual life into art is that spiritual science must not remain abstract theory or teaching but must be made part of actual life and take practical effect there. It was strikingly evident in these Munich performances that it is not the aim of spiritual science to achieve this by external subtlety or cleverness, but that its very life can pour vigor into that of art. This was proved by the whole-heartedness and growing understanding with which anthroposophists who were present in Munich threw themselves into the work. It is also evident from the fact that in the year 1909 we gave one dramatic performance, two last year, and this year—in spite of great difficulties—we were able to prepare three performances. If you study deeply enough, a work like *The Soul's Probation*† will indicate to you that occult observations, just as those of external life, can be presented in artistic form. If it were a matter of speaking about the essence of these things, I should have a very great deal to say.

What is particularly striking in these Munich gatherings is the steady increase in the number of those who throng to the meetings, with the result that we are becoming acutely conscious of the lack of space, not only for the performances but also for the lectures. During the lecture course, this lack of space was such that the heat of the hall caused great discomfort to the listeners. The obvious answer would be to take a larger hall. But there is a difficulty there too. As you all know, spiritual science calls for a certain intimacy. It would be highly inappropriate to produce one of the old Greek dramas in a circus stadium. (According to reliable reports, this has been done recently, although nothing but an entire absence of understanding for art could win for it any general approval or encouragement. One cannot help being astounded that such a thing has been thought possible . . . but, after all, it is not to be wondered at when we realize how greatly our age lacks true feeling for art.) Inappropriate as it would be to produce an old Greek Drama in a circus stadium (I do not mean in an actual circus, of course), such premises would be equally inappropriate for spiritual science. An ancient Greek theater might be suitable, but not a vast stadium. I must confess that the size of the hall of the Architektenhaus† in Berlin seems to me to be the maximum, and instead of taking a still larger hall, I would much prefer to give a lecture twice over in the Architektenhaus than once in a still larger hall. These things are so connected with the innermost character of spiritual science that they may not be understood today, but it will be different when spiritual science finds its way into the many domains and spheres of life.

Now in connection with our activities in Munich—if through what can be done in one hall, anything worthy of anthroposophy is to be achieved—we have come, inevitably, to the conclusion that we must create our own premises and surroundings. This has led to the idea of erecting a building in Munich† which would enable us to have a hall of our own, adequate for the needs of the gatherings there. The near future will show whether such a project will meet with success. For this much is certain: if we do find the way clear to erect a building in Munich, it must be done soon; otherwise the finest results of our work will be lost, precisely because during the next few years it will be possible to carry on our work adequately, provided only we have the space. That something is really achieved by building our own premises—this we have seen, not only in various small beginnings, but now again in Stuttgart, where the group has built the first house for anthroposophy existing in Central Europe.† Those who were present at its opening will have been amply convinced of what it means to have premises that are dedicated to anthroposophical work, and how completely different it is to go into such a room, compared with other rooms—quite apart from the details of which I spoke at the Opening, in connection with the significance of color, the shaping of the space, and so on, for the cultivation of spiritual knowledge.

Many ears, hearts, and souls are open to receive the deepening for which we are striving in anthroposophy, and there will be many, many more. We have seen, too—indeed it is constantly forced upon us—how eager people are to acquire knowledge of the spiritual world by an easy path. I believe that as the necessity for a deepening of thought and feeling, a widening of knowledge in the different domains of life, and in the occult life too, is brought home in course after course of lectures, many who have worked with us will already have discovered that in our stream of spiritual life, things are not made too easy. When we think of all the literature that has accumulated through the years—and I am sometimes appalled at the number of lecture courses and publications piled on our book tables—literature with which every sincere member desires to make himself intimately acquainted, or at any rate must study to some extent—when we think about this, we may truly say that we do not make it easy for anybody to reach the spiritual world. And yet as the years go by, it is more and more evident that ears and hearts and souls of human beings are open, whenever we have been able to approach them. Although for strange reasons into which we will not enter now, the Congress of the European Sections of the Theosophical Society in Genoa fell through, our own activities did not cease on that account. When the Congress was abandoned (its cancellation was announced only at the last minute and we will speak of the reasons later on), some people might have thought that we could still have held meetings, but it became evident at once that the time must be put to a different use. And so during the days that had been fixed for the Genoa Congress, lectures were given in Lugano, Locarno, Milan, Neuchâtel, and Berne.[†] We were able, therefore, to work during this time in places which it would have been difficult to visit in the near future. In Neuchâtel, a group was founded, desiring to adopt the name of a great spiritual individuality, Christian Rosenkreutz, of whom the members were eager to hear more intimate details. (I will shortly give a lecture on this subject here too.) When it is remembered that in order to speak about Christian Rosenkreutz at all, in order to understand this mysterious individuality, all the occult truths gathered in the course of many years are required and that there was a real longing for a more intimate knowledge, then it is clear that understanding of spiritual science has been deepened, although it has not been made easy for those who are working with us. And yet, on the other hand, how easy it is made, in reality, for those who sincerely strive for this deepening—how easy it is made! It may be said without boasting that it is made easy for them.

Think, for example, about the following. I have said repeatedly that, in our movement, the basis of anthroposophical life must be this occult ideal: There is in reality only one true form of occultism. To distinguish between an "Eastern" and a "Western" occultism would make as much sense as to distinguish between Eastern and Western mathematics. But on account of intrinsic characteristics, one kind of problem falls more readily into the sphere of occultism in the East and another into that of occultism in the West. Everything that relates to the great Appearance of which we have been speaking for years as the Appearance of Christ, is the result of the occult investigations pursued during recent centuries in the European esoteric schools, the European centers of occultism. All that has been said concerning the individuality known to us as "Jesus of Nazareth," concerning the two Jesus boys, the descent of Christ into the body of Jesus of Nazareth at the time of the Baptism by John in the river Jordan, concerning the Mystery of Golgotha and now recently, in Carlsruhe, concerning the Mystery of the Resurrection[†]—all these are truths which could not have been given out today were it not for the occult investigations which have continued in the West from the twelfth century down to the present time. Christianity cannot be understood without knowledge of these truths. Nobody—however great a theologian he may be—can understand Christianity unless he understands the Resurrection, for example. Those who speak like the theologians of today simply cannot understand Christianity—for what can they make of the words of St. Paul[†]: "If Christ be not risen, then is our preaching vain, and your faith also is vain"? In short, where there is no understanding of the Resurrection, there can be no understanding of Christianity! On the other hand, it must also be remembered that the intellect as such, whether directed to spiritual or to natural science, is incapable of approaching subjects like the Resurrection. A modern thinker will say that he must abandon the whole structure of his thought if he is really to believe in the Resurrection and what is described in the Gospel of John. Many people have realized and said as much. It is therefore necessary for light to be shed on these things by occultism in the West. So far as can be known from outside, the trend of occultism pursued in the East does not cover these particular truths, which are connected with the mysteries of the West, with the mysteries of Christianity. And why? Over in Asia, with the exception of regions in and around Asia Minor, people are not, and have not been, interested in Christ. They do not feel the need to ask about Him, nor have they done so for hundreds and thousands of years. In India and in Tibet, wonderful occult teachings exist about the Buddha and the Bodhisattvas, but nobody has been particularly interested in occult research concerning the being of Christ. The oriental school of theosophy cannot, therefore, be expected to have any real knowledge of the Christ.

You all know of the tremendous service rendered by H. P. Blavatsky† to the theosophical movement when it first came into being. Did the greatness of her achievement consist in formulating the three "principles" of the Theosophical Society, which are still printed on our forms of application for membership? It certainly did not lie in the statement that there must be a society for the cultivation of Universal Brotherhood! There are many such societies and every normal, thinking person will approve of the cultivation of Universal Brotherhood. The greatness of H. P. Blavatsky's work lay in the fact that, through her, an untold number of occult truths found their way into the world. Anyone who studies *Isis Unveiled* and then *The Secret Doctrine*, which appeared years later, will realize that in spite of everything that can be said against these works, they do, nevertheless, contain countless truths, truths of which, until then, nobody except those who had experienced initiation had any inkling. Although Madame Blavatsky had an illogical, disorderly mind, although her own speculations are placed, inappropriately, side by side with communications from the Masters (to go into this now would lead too far), although she was passionate and impetuous and often said things she should not have said (for it is not legitimate in occultism to speak so passionately and illogically), although it might be considered advisable to get some system and logical sequence into *Isis Unveiled*, or to eliminate five-sixths of *The Secret Doctrine* and edit the remaining sixth, yet in the theosophical life we must look at the positive side and say that a great and powerful impulse was there brought into the occult life.

The truth of these matters is that when H.P. Blavatsky wrote *Isis Unveiled*, she was under a kind of Rosicrucian inspiration. *Isis Unveiled* contains great Rosicrucian truths—even the shortcomings of Rosicrucianism are included. Everything of real importance in the book is Rosicrucian. I said "even the shortcomings of Rosicrucianism" because insight into the truths of reincarnation and karma, for instance, was not possible in the old Rosicrucianism of the thirteenth, fourteenth, and fifteenth centuries. It was only later on that they could be recognized in the West. In *Isis Unveiled*, Madame Blavatsky gave nothing that even approximates to an adequate explanation of reincarnation and karma; in short, she took over all the shortcomings of Rosicrucianism. Then it came about that through circumstances to describe which would lead too far, Madame Blavatsky fell away from the Rosicrucian influences and was enticed into an oriental form of theosophy.[†] The outcome of this was *The Secret Doctrine*, which in regard to everything that is not connected with Christianity contains great truths, but the greatest nonsense in regard to Christianity. Concerning the various religions and systems of thought in the world—with the exception of Judaism and Christianity—*The Secret Doctrine* is very useful, but nothing the book says about Judaism and Christianity is of the slightest value because H. P. Blavatsky had entered a sphere in which the truths in these two religions had not been cultivated. The whole direction subsequently taken by the theosophical movement is connected with this. The theosophical movement proved incapable of any real understanding of Christianity. Let me make it clear, by an example that is important for us, how the theosophical movement has failed in this respect.

In oriental occultism—apart from its very highest initiates, who do not speak otherwise than we—the loftiest individuality is that of the Bodhisattva. One such Bodhisattva was the individuality who, about five hundred years before our era, rose to the next rank, which again is understood in orientalism. In his twenty-ninth year, the Bodhisattva who had been born as the son of King Suddhodana became the Buddha. The attainment of Buddhahood, as everyone conversant with Buddhism understands, means that the being in question, after the physical life during which he has become Buddha, can never again appear on the earth. When the Bodhisattva becomes Buddha, he no longer returns to the Earth in an ordinary body, nor is he subject to the laws of reincarnation. But he has a "successor." When the Bodhisattva received Enlightenment and rose to Buddhahood, he "nominated" a successor to become Bodhisattva. This next Bodhisattva will be born as a human being, a human being towering above others, until he himself ascends to the rank of Buddha. It is known to every true disciple of orientalism that exactly five thousand years after the Enlightenment of Gautama Buddha under the Bodhi Tree, the Bodhisattva succeeding him will attain to Buddhahood and will appear as Maitreya Buddha—in three thousand years' time from now. Up to then a Bodhisattva will live in manifold incarnations yet to come; he will appear again and again on the earth, but will not rise to the rank of Buddha for another three thousand years—and then he will be a great teacher on the earth.

This is the highest individuality recognized by oriental occultism. Because Madame Blavatsky had been captured, as it were, by the oriental trend of occultism, such understanding of these things as might have been attained was limited by Eastern conceptions. At the same time, also, there was the desire to bring to Europeans further light on Christianity; but no real understanding of Christianity was possible by means of Eastern teachings—for they lead only to the individualities of the Bodhisattva and the Buddha. The consequence of this was that even those who were endowed with clairvoyance could only perceive the individuality of a Bodhisattva. A Bodhisattva was, however, incarnated in Jeshu ben Pandira, who lived 105 years before our era. He was closely connected with the Essenes and had pupils, among them one who was afterwards responsible for the Gospel of Matthew. A Bodhisattva individuality, the successor of Gautama Buddha, was incarnated in Jeshu ben Pandira, of whom oriental theosophy speaks. And to clairvoyant vision, it seemed as though nothing of particular importance happened 105 years after Jeshu ben Pandira had lived. Think of H. P. Blavatsky. She directed her occult gaze to the time when Jeshu ben Pandira was living and saw that a great Bodhisattva individuality was incarnated in him. But because her entanglement in an oriental trend of theosophy had limited her powers of vision, she was incapable of seeing that 105 years afterwards, the *Christ* had come. Of Christ she knew only what was said in the West, and from this she conceived the notion that no "Christ" ever lived, that it was all make-believe; but that 105 years before our era there had lived a certain Jeshu ben Pandira, who was stoned and then hanged on a tree—who was not, therefore, crucified. Jeshu ben Pandira was now described as if *he* had been Jesus of Nazareth. This is a complete confusion. Concerning the real Jesus of Nazareth who was the Bearer of the Christ, nothing is said. Jeshu ben Pandira, who had lived 105 years earlier, was said to be "Christ," because a European name was thought to be desirable.

We, however, are obliged to say that those who stand within that oriental stream do not perceive who the Christ-being is. It cannot be denied that the moment attention has to be drawn to a matter like this, we find ourselves in an unpleasant position. And why? Everyone who is acquainted with the sciences knows that there are matters which can be disputed; but there are others which cannot be disputed—and there, if someone holds a contrary opinion, it can only be said that he does not understand the point at issue. Now if we say, "You do not understand this," we may be considered extremely arrogant! We are in this unpleasant position in that we cannot agree with those who speak of Jeshu ben Pandira as the "Christ." The fact is that they simply have not reached the stage of being able to understand. It is unpleasant to have to say this, but it is a fact. They are really not to be blamed when they speak of the being, whom they too recognize, as though he could come again and again in the body—for they have no real knowledge of the Christ-being who could appear only once in the flesh! And now take *Esoteric Christianity* by Annie Besant,† and read it with more care than is usual in theosophical circles. It speaks of an individuality who lived 105 years before our era; but the mistake is that *he* is called "Christ." Suppose some person—the author of this book, for instance—were now to say that during the twentieth century, the being described in *Esoteric Christianity* is to appear in some human being in the flesh. Nothing more could be said against this, from our standpoint, than would be said to anyone who might go to India and proclaim that the Buddha will incarnate again. He would be told: "You are an ignorant European! Everyone knows that the Buddha can never appear again in the flesh; you therefore understand nothing about Buddhism." But we, too, in Europe must be entitled to take the same attitude when it is alleged that Christ will incarnate a second time! Our reply can only be: "You do not understand. True knowledge of the Christ-being reveals that he is a being who can appear once, and once only, in a body of flesh." Let us say that understanding here lies on different levels; then there can be no misunderstanding!

What is the point that might really separate us from an oriental trend of theosophy? Do we deny that a man lived 105 years before our era, who was stoned for blasphemy and afterwards hanged on a tree? No, we do not deny it. Or do we deny that a great individuality dwelt in that being? We do not. Neither do we deny that this being may reincarnate in the twentieth century. We admit it. Is there therefore any real issue concerning which we should have to repudiate the statements made by the other school of theosophy? Only this, that we are bound to say: "You do not know the being whom we call Christ; you call another by his name." We must have the right to correct this. As for the rest, it is only a question of nomenclature, except when you expressly ignore matters of which we speak in connection with the beginning of our era. We speak of the two Jesus children, the Baptism by John in the Jordan, the Mystery of Golgotha. Of these, you say nothing! We must be allowed the right to know things of which you are ignorant! Otherwise, one would be under the decree: "What we do not know, nobody else has the right to know; for what we do not know is all false!" In this connection, our position is that we do not make the trouble, and when any is made, it is the others who are responsible for it.

All misunderstandings could very easily be avoided. So far as we are concerned there is no reason for misunderstanding, and none exists. Only we must have the right to bring to theosophical life the results of occult researches of which nothing is known on the other side, and which immeasurably deepen our understanding of the problems of the West. So in one important respect, provided only that good will exists, it is not in the least necessary for disharmony to arise in the theosophical movement. Good will is necessary—not the attitude that is ready to repudiate some authenticated truth—for that would not be good will but denial of truth! Good will must be accompanied by reason. Why do differences of opinion arise? Is it because some subject is looked at from different standpoints or also, possibly, from different levels? If the latter is the case, the others will not be able to substantiate their opinion. And then it is a matter of realizing how the land lies, and of having tolerance.

For us, at any rate, this principle must be established, and I had to refer to it on this first occasion when we are together again. I have referred to it as a proof that in our movement it is very easy to see things clearly if there is a sincere wish to do so. We ourselves may truly say that there is no need for us to oppose anyone. We can afford to wait until the opposition comes from elsewhere. We can go on working quietly, and this subject would not have been raised or mentioned at all, if friends had not been distressed by the rumor that theosophists are all at variance among themselves. It is true that, ultimately, we may find ourselves in the very disagreeable position of being obliged to say: "On the other side, they have no knowledge of certain truths." This may lead to an accusation of arrogance, but we can put up with that, provided we know what real humility is.

During this last year, it has been necessary to give expression to the progress—for so it may truly be called—that has taken place in occult investigation since the middle of the thirteenth century. This has been done, for instance, in my book *The Spiritual Guidance of the Individual and Humanity.*[†] These developments are hardly mentioned in any movement other than our own. It may be said, therefore, that we have had to undertake the difficult task of assimilating the most recent results of occult research. It may be regarded as a good augury that at the founding of the Neuchâtel group, the need was expressed for more intimate knowledge of the greatest teacher of Christianity[†]—Christian Rosenkreutz—of his incarnations and of the nature of his work. I have spoken as I have today in order that each of you may know how things really are, when someone on the other side says: "Here we are told that Christ will incarnate again in the twentieth century, but over there it is said that he will appear as a spiritual being only. These are two conflicting standpoints." No, we must not allow this to be said. It must, however, be emphasized—and admitted by the other side, too—that they are speaking of Jeshu ben Pandira, who was stoned 105 years before our era. When, for instance, in

Annie Besant's last book, *The Changing World*,† everything is jumbled up and no mention made of the usurpation of the name "Christ," when sheer contradiction exists between *Esoteric Christianity* and *The Changing World*, these are matters which really must be pointed out in order to prevent people from being misled into thinking that in her latest book Annie Besant is speaking of the real Christ. If this were so, she would have to repudiate the book *Esoteric Christianity* and say that its contents are not correct—for that book speaks of a being who lived 105 years before our era, not at its beginning.

Our work is characterized by the fact that the findings of occult investigation cover even the most modern times. From one point of view, therefore, it is a kind of aspersion—although an unintentional one—when outsiders call us "Rosicrucians." It really is a kind of aspersion: at any rate it reminds me of an amusing incident which once took place in the market of a town in central Germany. One man said: "So-and-so is a sluggard." "What?" said another, "you say he is a sluggard? But I know that he is a butcher, not a sluggard!" The same kind of logic which implies that if a man is a butcher, he cannot be a sluggard underlies assertions to the effect that our movement is not "theosophical" but "Rosicrucian." Why do we cultivate Rosicrucian principles? Because genuine Rosicrucian schools of occultism have existed and because the results of Rosicrucian knowledge must be received into our own movement—just as we have spoken, without any bias whatever, about Brahmanism, orientalism, about ancient and modern Christianity. I do not think that in many other theosophical groups mention has been made, for instance, of the Mexican deities Quetzalcoatl and Tezcatlipoca,† as has been done among us. So, in addition to all the other subjects, we have also included the results reached by genuine Rosicrucian investigation—naturally so, since we do not disdain the fruits of genuine occultism. If we have become familiar with a number of symbols derived from Rosicrucianism, it is because they have the best influence upon the minds and hearts of modern people. We are "modern" theosophists precisely because we do not refuse to accept the results of the most modern research. Perhaps someone has heard that I have sometimes used the form of address: "My dear Rosicrucian friends." These things occur just because we stand upon the universal foundations of theosophy. It is, therefore, an unconscious aspersion when the designation "Rosicrucian" is imposed upon our movement. We must, however, be tolerant about these things.

Our task this winter will be to deepen still further the teachings and truths already received. And so, in order to prepare the ground for speaking about Christian Rosenkreutz here,[†] too, I want to speak about the threefold nature of man and its true basis, in so far as man is a being capable of receiving intellectual, aesthetic, and moral impulses. We shall have to search very deeply into the occult foundations of these things, and expand the teachings already received—for instance, about the Saturn, Sun, and Moon evolutions—by studying man as an intellectual, an aesthetic, and a moral being.

Lecture Two

BERLIN, MARCH 19, 1912

As an introduction, I would like to tell you two short stories. The first (I will omit certain details) is as follows:

Once upon a time, there lived two boys who from earliest childhood had been close friends. One of them was outstandingly gifted, learned with extraordinary facility, and as he grew older, he gave every promise of attaining high academic honors. The other boy was much less talented. His friend, who was deeply attached to him, taught and helped him in every way, but he was incapable of learning very much. This, however, did not greatly affect his circumstances as a small inheritance provided for his living. The more gifted boy grew to adolescence but when he was on the point of getting a university degree, he died. As in the country where these young men lived it was customary to marry and start a family very early in life, it devolved upon the other, less gifted youth to provide for the family of the friend who had died. This he did, but before long his own means were exhausted. He said to himself: "As my friend's talents have proved so transient, my mundane possessions, too, will probably soon have disappeared; I must set about making a living." This he did by becoming a travelling merchant. Once, when he was sitting in front of a house in a strange neighborhood, a gigantic man came and sat down beside him. He gave the impression of not having eaten anything for days and seemed to be famished with hunger. The other took compassion on him and ordered a meal to be brought. It was very quickly consumed, to the astonishment of the merchant, but as the one meal was not enough to appease the other's hunger, he ordered a second. The big man ate this just as ravenously and then said that to satisfy his hunger he must have a whole ham and a number of cakes. He devoured all these and, after his enormous meal, seemed satisfied. This incident led to friendship between the big man and the little man, and they set out together on their travels. Very soon, however, the little man found the big man something of a burden and told him that he could well dispense with his company. The big man, however, assured the little man of his friendship, saying that he would never forsake him, in sorrow or in joy. The little man now felt a wish to question the big man about his life, and the latter replied: "I have no house on the earth, no boat on the sea; by day I live in the village, by night in the town." To begin with, the little man had no notion of what this meant. Then it happened that they had to cross a wide river. Their boat capsized and sank, and both fell into the water. The big man extricated himself very quickly, carried the little man to a safe spot, brought up the boat and put the little man into it, then he dived again into the water and brought up all the goods, even the tiniest articles, which the little man was intending to trade. This naturally aroused in the little man the greatest respect for the other, and as friends they had many talks together, sometimes on profound subjects. Thus on one occasion the little man said to the big man: "Oh! If only one could rise consciously to heaven; if only it were possible to know what is going on up there!" Thereupon the big man answered him: "Maybe you would like to soar into the air," and when the little man had assented, he very soon became aware of fatigue and fell asleep. When he woke up, the stars were above him, like pollen in the cup of a lotus-flower in heaven; he was even able to pluck one of these flowers, hiding it in his sleeve. Then he saw a great ship approaching, drawn and steered by dragons. In it was a great vessel of water, and the big man, who was with the little man in the clouds, showed him how the water could be poured out and allowed to trickle down to the earth. Then the little man realized that he was able to act as do the spirits of the air, when they let the rain pour down upon the earth. He begged the big man to pour the water in the vessel on his native soil and to let him go down again to the earth by a rope. The big man said to him: "Now you have rescued me; I am a son of the thunder god, and my duty has been to bestow rain and other blessings upon the earth. Because for a time I did not perform my duty properly, I was obliged to lead on earth the life of which you know." Then he let the little man go down again to the earth. The latter was now in his home once more, having with him the star he had gathered in the meadow of heaven. This he placed upon the table and it filled the whole room with miraculous light, strong enough even to read by. During the day, it looked like a simple meteorite, but at night it was radiant and luminous. This continued until one night the little man's wife, rather a vain woman, was combing her hair by its light. This displeased the star-stone and it shrank to a tiny size. One day the wife had a strange impulse to swallow the stone! Thereupon there came to the little man a vision of the big man whom he knew so intimately, and the latter said to him: "Owing to what has happened now, I can reach a particular stage of development. Now I shall be able to come to the earth for a time as a son of the thunder god. Your wife will bear me as your son." And he was actually born as the son of the little man. A peculiarity of this child was that in the dark he shone like a star, so that people called him the "Star Child." He lived on, and although as he grew older his radiance waned, it still revealed itself in the form of his great talents. Very soon he became a man of high importance in life.

This is the one story. You will wonder why I am telling you these tales, but before answering, I will tell you a second, very similar one.

Once upon a time there lived a man who, in our country, might rank as a "Councilor" or "Governor." He and his family lived in a spacious, very beautiful house. But after a time, strange things began to happen there. By day, and especially by night, nobody in it could get any rest; they were always being knocked, pinched, and dragged about in all directions; objects were hurled at them and the house swarmed with ghosts. Because of this, the family left the house and went to another, leaving a servant behind as caretaker; but after a few days, he died. They sent a second and then a third, both of whom also died. They then decided to leave the house without any servant at all. A young sceptic now turned up, a youth who was preparing for an examination, and he wanted to take the house for his studies. The Councilor warned him that he would probably never come out alive, and that at any rate terrible things happened to everyone in the house. But the young man replied: "I have written a treatise on the very subject of the 'Unreality of Spirits,' proving that they do not exist. I could write a great many more and nobody who has written about such matters is in the least afraid of what may happen in such a house!" So the Councilor was prevailed upon to let him have the house. The young man took with him masses of books to study and sat down to begin his work. It was not long, however, before one of his ears was pinched, then the other; then he was attacked somewhere else and molested in all sorts of ways. When he went to bed, the trouble began in real earnest! He could get no rest the whole night long and, sceptic though he was, he began to be dreadfully frightened. Nevertheless, he refused to give way to terror and held out valiantly. On account of his power of endurance, the spectral figures who were wont to bend over his books and play pranks by closing his eyes when he wanted to read, and so on, revealed themselves to him. This heartened the brave young man considerably, but it was a really ghastly state of affairs. Things went on like this until his good-heartedness enabled him to set up a kind of friendship with two spirit-beings who were always annoying and molesting him. After a time, he discovered that the spirit-beings could not read but would like to be able to do so. And so, it came about that he established a kind of school for the spirits, teaching them how to copy out all sorts of things from his books. Not only were the spirits extremely grateful for this, but they had actually learnt something. Communication with the spirits was now quite a pastime for the young man, and the spirits who lived in the house had, moreover, profited greatly through him. The time came for his examination; as well as having had a great deal of amusement, he had imbibed so much knowledge that he was hopeful of passing, but the intrigues of an enemy caused the rumor that he had cheated in his written papers. As in that country the rules about such matters were extremely strict and because to begin with the rumor was believed, he was sent to prison and retained there for some time with nothing to eat. Finally, however, one of his spirit-friends brought food to him. She then began to bring the other spirits with her and they provided for all his needs. Thus there grew up between the young man and one of his spirit-friends a friendship much greater even than it had been before. And after his innocence had been established and he had been set free, although he had formerly "proved the unreality of spirits," his spirit-friend was now such a reality to him that he resolved to marry her! She answered, however, that situated as she was, she could not marry, for she belonged to the spiritual worlds, but that if he would go to a certain priest-magician and ask his advice, there would be a way out of the dilemma. So he went to the priest-magician, who gave him a charm, saying that if, when a funeral was passing, his spirit-friend would go to the coffin and swallow this charm, she could then become a human being and marry him. Not long afterwards a funeral was actually taking place. The spirit-friend approached the procession, swallowed the charm and then and there disappeared into the coffin. People were astounded in the highest degree when the figure they had seen disappeared into the coffin (for when she had swallowed the charm she became visible). They therefore put the coffin on the ground, opened it, and found that it contained no body at all! The burial could not, therefore, take place. But after a few days, the spirit-friend came to the young man, told him that she had now become a human being—the one who had been in the coffin—and that they could now enter into wedlock. And so the two whose acquaintance had begun in the haunted house, now lived on in the companionship of marriage.

*

If you give some thought to these two stories, you will have to admit that however close a search you may make in the literature accessible to Europeans, right back to the time when there was universal belief in ghosts, no such stories will be found. You will find indications of how the spirit world plays into the world of men—but stories of this kind, giving the feeling that there could be no more natural and spontaneous way of depicting the interplay between the spirit world and the human world, simply do not exist in European literature. They are quite unique. A curious feature strikes us when we study their composition. In the first story, we are told, for instance, that a star is born as the son of a human being and goes on living as a man upon the earth. To the kind of consciousness underlying the first story, it is a natural matter of course that beings exist in the stars, beings who are the primordial kith and kin of men, and that those who walk the earth as men may, in reality, be embodied star-beings. This underlies the first story as a natural and accepted fact. In the second, a human being who enters into actual wedlock with another, first came to know her in the spiritual world; she then descends into the physical world and her life continues there. The trend of the two stories is identical. This sense of "togetherness" with the spiritual world—not in the form in which it is expressed in European sagas and legends, but on the totally different ground of which we shall presently speak—will nowhere be found, in the same peculiar form, in the literature of Europe—except if it were to be imitated by some modern writer.

And now remind yourselves of something I said in one of the last public lectures.[†] In the way that is possible in such a lecture, I spoke about the beginnings of Earth evolution and of the genesis of man in connection with Earth evolution. I said that the process of the evolution of *humanity* began at a comparatively late stage. We ourselves speak of the evolution of man and of mankind in the following way. When a human being is to enter physical existence on the earth, the innermost kernel or core of his being works within a certain field of activity, molding the finer organs, the brain, and the more delicate bodily tissues. Thus there is in man an essential soul-spiritual core which passes over from earlier incarnations, envelops itself in what comes from the forefathers, and is carried through the generations by the process of physical heredity. In a human being who appears on the earth, a union takes place between what comes from earlier incarnations and what is carried through the generations, enveloping that which passes from incarnation to incarnation. I said that this form of the evolutionary process began only during the Atlantean epoch, when conditions rendering such a development possible arose for the first time on the earth. I indicated that this particular process of evolution had been preceded by another, in which the human being did not pass into earthly existence by way of union between man and woman and then the descent of the soul which passes through the several incarnations. In very early periods of Earth evolution, the human being originated in an altogether different way. The reason for this is that not until the *post*-Atlantean period did Earth actually resemble its present configuration. In the last Atlantean epoch, the Earth did not really differ, in essentials, from what it is at present; but the *early* Atlantean epoch was fundamentally different from the later, and anyone who ignores the fact that at that time entirely other conditions prevailed has a totally false conception of the configuration of the Earth. After having passed through the periods of Old Saturn, Old Sun, and Old Moon, the Earth was not only a living organism, but also a spiritual being, a great organism permeated by spirit and soul. We do not get back to an inanimate ball of gas as intimated by the Kant-Laplace theory, but to the Earth as a huge, living being. In that ancient time, the evolutionary process of humanity was such that fertilization did not take place between man and woman but between the "above" and the "below"—in the sense that the Earth with its forces of life provided the element of substance, the more material element, whereas the spiritual principle came from above, like rain which fertilizes the soil of meadows, and united with the more material principle. It was by this method of fertilization that the first human beings came into existence. This was indicated in the public lecture and can be established on logical grounds if one views the achievements of natural science in the right light.

Then the Earth separated out from itself a solid mass, like a kind of bony system, and it was impossible thereafter for it to provide, as before, the substance for fertilization. The process had now to take place *within* the human organism. Instead of the fertilization "from above," fertilization now came about by way of the two sexes, and the process which had formerly been set in train by interaction between the "above" and the "below" now passed over into the operations of heredity and into those of reincarnation, which are bound up with heredity. Thus what had taken place on the surface of the Earth in earlier times had now passed *into* the being of man. Human beings came into existence and were able, in the sense of a continuous hereditary reproduction, to inherit or carry over from one incarnation to the next those qualities which had formerly been received directly from the spiritual world. As was said in the public lecture, the very first human beings were hermaphrodites, then there was differentiation into the male and the female, and then a gradual development into the conditions prevailing at present; what in earlier times had operated more from above—the female element—passed into the woman, and what had operated more in the earthly element passed over in the stream of heredity into the male.

From intimations given through the course of years concerning the evolution of humanity, you will have realized that these conditions prevailed right on into the Atlantean epoch; it was not until the second half of the Atlantean epoch that the evolutionary process assumed, more or less, its present form. The Atlantean peoples on the Earth were really living in the aftermath of still earlier conditions, when the substantiality of the Earth was fertilized by the spirituality of the heavens. The Atlantean peoples saw the birth of a human being as a direct embodiment of the spiritual, a descent of the spiritual into the material. As we today see the rain falling from heaven and moistening the earth, so did the people of Atlantis see human beings coming down from heavenly heights, uniting with substance provided by the Earth and then wandering over its surface. Conditions changed only by slow degrees; in certain regions the preparatory stages of conditions as they are at present had long since been in existence, whereas in other regions where the old conditions had persisted, the Atlantean peoples knew that the human being exists, to begin with, in the spiritual world and then seeks bodily substance in order to become part of Earth humanity. Thus when a human being in Atlantean times saw his contemporaries moving about the earth, he said to himself: "The form I see there derives from the Earth, but what is within it derives from the same world to which the stars belong: the human being has descended from the worlds of the stars!" It sounds like a fairy-tale echoing from olden time. Man comes down from heavenly heights, surrounds and clothes himself with earthly substance. The Atlantean peoples knew of the interaction between the Heavens and the Earth. They knew: To begin with, man is a spirit; then he descends, clothes himself in matter and moves about the Earth. Man was seen as a heavenly being, a being from the spiritual world. For it was known that as he moved about, he differed from the spirits only in that he was clothed in matter. The transition from the spiritual world to the physical world was a much gentler, more delicate process. Not that the Atlantean would in any sense have denied the existence of the spiritual world. On the contrary, he saw clearly that there was no very essential difference between physical human beings and the spirit beings who belong to that other world. He knew: One can communicate with a human being through signs, by employing the early rudiments of human speech, and with the spirits, too, for the way in which man communicates with the spirits does not differ from the way he communicates with other human beings.

Naturally, only very little of this direct knowledge of man's connection with the spiritual world survived the Atlantean catastrophe. The mission of the *post-Atlantean* period was to develop in man an understanding of Earth existence proper, of all that can be acquired by the development of the body as a physical instrument. And so, the perfectly natural communion with the spiritual world very soon ceased in the course of the post-Atlantean period. But what disappeared from the *normal* consciousness was preserved in those periods or moments of atavistic clairvoyance when the soul withdrew more into itself. What in earlier times had been actual *experience* when the soul turned its gaze to the surrounding spiritual world was born again later on in the form of imagination, phantasy. Let us assume that in some particular people belonging to the post-Atlantean age, the characteristics and faculties of the Atlantean age still survived, more strongly than in all the others. Naturally, this people would not be able to have the experiences of Atlantis during the post-Atlantean age. But something would have to arise in the imagination of this people that distinguished it from the imagination of the remnants of Atlantean races[†] that had not stayed behind to the same degree and had been newly formed. The races that set the tone for the post-Atlantean period will therefore allow less to arise of this self-evident relationship of man with the spiritual worlds. A people, on the other hand, that is characterized by the fact that it can bring, as it were, into the post-Atlantean period what can be brought as soul constitution out of the Atlantean period—such a people must show entirely different aftereffects in the soul than the actual post-Atlantean races. With a people that could be characterized, in the sense of the occult world-view, as not belonging to the progressing races, but rather presents itself like something that remained behind from the old Atlantean race, with such a people we would have to suppose that the imagination, which speaks of the relationship between the world of humans and the world of ghosts, acts in an entirely different way than it does with other peoples. In the case of such a people, we could suppose that in a strange way something could arise in the imagination like the being of a star who suddenly decides to incarnate as the son of a human being who has rendered a service to the star, as it was described in our first novelistic story, where we saw that a star being—the son of the thunder god—was born as the son of the friend with whom he had for a time wandered the earth.

The second story suggests the gentler transition—a human being falls in love with a spirit being from above; such a being does not descend to human existence in the ordinary way but chooses a dead body. It is as though an Atlantean soul, accustomed to seeing human beings descend and take on earthly substance, had gone astray by choosing a body which was suitable not for the post-Atlantean epoch but for that of Atlantis, when human beings were not born as they now are but merely assumed a mantle of earthly substance. In the light of this interpretation, we can perceive in such stories the aftermath of earlier conditions. We would then not be surprised by such stories in the case of a race that was a remnant of earlier Atlantean races. It is interesting that a number of similar stories has been collected by Martin Buber[†] and published by Rütten and Loening in Frankfurt-am-Main under the title *Chinesische Geister- und Liebesgeschichten* [Chinese ghost and love stories].

All this indicates that what may be surmised from a study of occult science is actual fact—although, of course, these things are now no more than tradition.

Light can be shed upon a great deal that comes our way in life, if only we have patience to study the more intimate connections of world evolution. People of the present day will often stand amazed at such things and will only begin to understand them when they realize that anyone who is cognizant of the more intimate connections of human evolution accepts them as self-evident. Understanding of spiritual science is not furthered by pedantic demands for "logical proof"; proof, after all, is useful only to those who are willing to believe what is asserted; it is useful only to those who can believe that it *is* proof. Nobody need believe in it at all—and then they are spared from believing anything! Spiritual science will be received into human souls because of increasing evidence that those laws of which knowledge can be acquired only along the occult path can be applied even in the most hidden recesses of spiritual and material culture. The treasures of wisdom will come into their own when more and more people have patience enough to observe the harmony between all the facts of existence to which a spiritual conception of the world is applied, and to realize that only in this way can there be a true explanation of things which must otherwise remain incomprehensible.

Thinking of all these matters, we shall be able to say that post-Atlantean civilization has its particular mission. Human beings who rightly understand their times will unfold the knowledge, will-activity, and qualities of heart to be acquired through the instrumentality of the body. In these domains there will be greater and greater progress—progress which, fundamentally, is connected with the phase of evolution stretching from the time of the Holy Rishis of India to the descent of the Christ-impulse into humanity. But side by side with this there has existed much that is like "imprisoned" spiritual treasure. The people of Europe were astonished in the highest degree at the vistas of spiritual life opened up by the discoveries concerning the wisdom of India, of ancient Persia, concerning the Krishna- or Brahman-culture, or the ancient Zoroastrian culture. In the older civilizations, there was, naturally, a deeper spirituality than in the products of later forms of knowledge. People in the West were astonished by what German scholarship in the first half of the nineteenth century disclosed concerning these ancient civilizations, were astonished at the light shed upon the wisdom of India by Friedrich Schlegel[†] and, later on, upon the wisdom of Persia. These disclosures were so astonishing that the deep influence exercised by oriental philosophy upon the minds of thinkers like Schopenhauer[†] or Eduard von Hartmann[†] is readily understandable. There we have the first expressions of the wonder and astonishment of the West at what is contained in these ancient civilizations as a kind of "imprisoned" spirituality.

We are now confronting another epoch, in which imprisoned spirituality in a different form will be capable of causing amazement in the West—namely, the spirituality that does not belong to the mission of post-Atlantean humanity, but has remained as an heirloom from earlier times, concealed until our own time in the Chinese wisdom of which the West hitherto has known practically nothing. Very little will be sufficient to enable what will happen over there to overwhelm the spiritual culture of the West—to such an extent indeed, that it might well forget its own mission, its own specific significance and task. As people live on into the future they will have to realize that from the Atlantean epoch there has survived upon our Earth an imprisoned spiritual wisdom and knowledge greater than anything revealed by the disclosures concerning the old Brahman and Zoroastrian civilizations; this wisdom will be unleashed when the spiritual life of China emerges from its concealment. Two things will have to be realized by those who turn their eyes towards the future. From over yonder there will flow a mighty stream of spiritual life, containing, even in external details, most wonderful teachings, although such teachings would in any case be available to those willing to penetrate into the spiritual life along the path revealed by spiritual science. If, however (to quote words used in a different connection by our friend Michael Bauer[†] at our General Meeting), the great majority of human beings pull nightcaps over their eyes in regard to what spiritual science has to offer, then one day, in a form unsuited to Western mentality, spiritual treasures will pour from Chinese culture, and this portion of humanity, in their amazement, will realize that the products of such culture cannot be grasped by the pedantic thought common in the West but only by deeper insight into the ancient Taoist culture which arose on the soil of the ancient Chinese civilization. Spiritual science often goes against the grain because, by its very nature, study of it will induce belief. Those who deliberately pull nightcaps over their eyes will be amazed, but, on the other hand, also rather relieved when, in spiritual science, they come across many things that have passed over into Chinese culture from Atlantean times. They will comfort themselves by saying:

"There is no need to *believe* in that, for what history has preserved is studied simply because it is of interest!" This is the attitude of the philologists and archaeologists. There is no need to believe in it; one can get hold of it by study and be exempt from having to "believe." But when the wisdom casts off its fetters over yonder, it will have another effect as well: its obvious and intrinsic greatness will shock and amaze. It will pour over what mankind has acquired in Christian culture in such a way that it will have to be seen in its true perspective, studied from the right point of view. The proper approach will be to say: This spirituality existed; in bygone ages it constituted the spiritual culture of our Earth. But every epoch has its own mission, and that of Western culture is to drink at the well-springs of the spiritual reality behind world existence, so that this spiritual reality is perceived behind the material world, behind what eyes can see and hands can grasp—as a revelation from the spiritual world. People will have to understand that their mission now belongs to a *different* age and that they must stand firm on the ground prepared by Christianity!

That is the other picture. People will joyfully receive what derives from olden times but will illumine it, vivify it with what the more recent, post-Atlantean, Christian culture has imparted to the soul. Weaklings, however, will say: "We will accept spirituality from whatever source it may come, for all that interests us is a sensational vista of the spiritual worlds." There may actually be neo-theosophists who will say: "The truth is not to be found through deep comprehension of the Christ-principle; it lies in what has been preserved by the Chinese, coming to light again when they bring forth the Atlantean wisdom hidden in the deepest strata of their souls." Europe might well be offered a new secret doctrine compiled from the truths of Chinese wisdom, which would then say: This modern theosophy ought to be modeled on a theosophy that did not seek to derive the source of spiritual life from Christian mysticism and Christian love but rather plagiarized—and rather poorly at that—the wisdom of ancient India, somewhat embellished by the wisdom of ancient Egypt. As for the weaklings, they will be just as eager for Chinese wisdom as for the spirituality which they think is opened up for them by the ancient or also by the "newly revealed" Indian wisdom. After all, to Europeans,

India is almost as remote as China; and if people are told of revelations made possible in China owing to certain forces having been set free, this may well seem more credible to them than that anything of the kind should have transpired in Berlin.

If we ponder over these things, we shall find the true balance between joyful acceptance of what has been preserved from ancient epochs of culture and a firm footing on the soil resulting from evolution through the ages. That heed shall be paid to the importance of maintaining this balance, is and will remain the constant care of the movement with which we identify ourselves. It is simply an untruth when here or there it is said that we are out to reject or ignore what is offered in the way of Indian spirituality, for example. It is an untruth, as everyone who has taken part in our work well knows; and it would be grievous if such untruths were to take root in the world in connection with our movement. Opinions that are at variance are easy to deal with; they soon balance themselves out. But inaccurate statements give rise to one misunderstanding after another, for it is the peculiarity of misunderstanding that it constantly gives birth to fresh misunderstandings! With this in mind, it must be our primary task to realize how far our own standpoint on the soil of Western spiritual life is justified in face of the other phases of human evolution. On the other hand, we must take care that everything we say about those other phases of evolution, about other forms of spirituality, is presented *honestly* and *truthfully*. Again and again, it must be repeated and realized by theosophists that even if much of the spiritual insight we have been able to gain goes under, its influence will remain! No matter what transpires, our work must be full of *sincerity*, *integrity*, and *truthfulness*. And if, in future times, all that people will be able to say of our particular work is that many a thing was improved, many another has not survived, but, nevertheless, it was an example of the fact that occultism and earnest spiritual research can be entirely free from charlatanism or humbug, that the striving for occult knowledge can be true, genuine, and sincere—if that can be said of us, we shall really have done something to further the development of the spiritual and occult movement! And it will perhaps be recognized as our greatest conscious awareness that we do not want to grant entry to anything about which one could not speak in this way.

Lecture Three

BERLIN, MARCH 26, 1912

We will begin the lecture today by thinking of what is implied by the word "chance." We say that certain happenings in the world are comprehensible to us because they take their course "in accordance with law"; in them we recognize certain laws, "natural laws." Of other happenings it is said that they seem to be governed by no law; the time at which they occur, the sequence of circumstances connected with them—all must be attributed to "chance." Modern science, recognizing only those abstract laws which it calls the "laws of nature," will certainly be prone, where these laws prove inapplicable, to speak of "mere chance," of something, that is to say, in regard to which conformity to law cannot be admitted. When modern science speaks of "chance" in cases to which its laws do not apply, it really puts a ban upon any suggestion of conformity to law. Both generally and in particulars, there is hardly anything more intolerant in human life than the "scientific attitude." I do not, of course, refer to scientific *facts*, for they are presented in a way which does science the very highest credit, and intolerance does not come into question here. I am speaking of the "scientific attitude" which arises on the foundation of these facts. The attitude of materialistic thought today is an example of almost the greatest intolerance to be found in history.

If, in the light of spiritual science, we consider "chance" in relation to the life of feeling, our first question will be: How does chance befall the human being? How does it present itself to him? When something happens "by chance," it seems as though the human being could not possibly, out of his own thoughts—whatever they may be—ascribe any meaning, any inner conformity to law, to this "chance" event. It looks as though reason must simply let it go at that, without bothering to ascertain whether any conformity to law could possibly be attributed to it. People are usually unwilling to bring reason or intelligence to bear upon unforeseen occurrences which, as such, are apparently quite inexplicable. Where *feeling* is concerned, however, the attitude is very different, although this is not generally realized. Feeling does not always allow itself to be dominated by intellectual preconceptions or by the reasoning mind, but rises out of hidden depths of the soul where man is wiser than he is in his intellect and reason. Thus it may well happen that in his life of feeling, a person is attracted or repelled, pleased or displeased by what his reason and intellect call "pure chance." We will take a definite example. A schoolboy is wrestling with a sum he has to solve; he pores over it and struggles hard but still cannot get it right. After persistent efforts, he solves it, to his great delight. But he says to himself: "To be quite certain that I have got it right and shall not be kept in and be given a bad mark, I must go through it all again." So he makes up his mind that after supper he will work it all out again. Then, quite by chance, and owing to entirely unrelated circumstances, a classmate turns up at his home and asks him what solution he has reached. They compare results and find that they agree. In this way the boy is spared from an additional strain; not needing to pore over the sum any longer, he is free and can go to bed at once. Now if the father is what is called an "enlightened" man, he will say: "The other boy did not call in unexpectedly just to save my boy an hour's study which might have injured his health, but was sent by his mother to bring something I had left behind." The father calls it "chance." But the boy has a feeling of happiness, although he will probably not go to the length of believing that an angel brought this school friend to him; the reaction of his feelings, at any rate, will be quite different from that of his reason and intellect. The father will certainly not be inclined to accept the idea that an angel from heaven sent the friend to his son, yet he too will feel glad about what happened.

That is what I mean when I say that when feeling rises out of hidden depths in the life of soul, it may well be cleverer than the intellect and the reasoning mind which have to develop independence in the course of the Earth's mission, to develop in such a way that they are thrown back entirely on themselves; reason and intellect are, so to speak, "God-forsaken," and can therefore easily fall into the error of believing that in what presents itself to them as chance, there is no divine-spiritual conformity to law, nor anything like it. Therefore, we may say that what rises out of the depths of the soul makes us—as in this case—cleverer in our feelings than we are in our life of intellect and reason. This indicates quite clearly that spiritual science is right when it asserts that what lies in the depths of the soul and rises in the feelings from these depths, originates from an epoch when the human being was not thrown back entirely upon himself; that the element of sympathy or antipathy in the life of soul is something that came over from the Old Moon period. Therefore, during the course of Earth evolution, the human being has to become as clever in his life of intellect and reason as he became in his life of feeling during the Old Moon period of evolution. Someone may say at this point: "But I have observed that feelings are by no means always clever; they can also be the very opposite!" The reason for this is that our feelings as human beings of Earth are influenced by the intellect which works down into the feelings. If our feelings are stupid, they have become so only because they have been influenced by the intellect. If the life of feeling had remained immune from this influence, despite the circumstances connected with incarnation and the general evolution of mankind, then the feelings would, in fact, be cleverer than the intellect and the reason.

Considered from this point of view, something of special interest concerning "chance" presents itself, something that is extremely instructive. The question might indeed be raised: "Is there not also significance in the very fact that certain things can be regarded as fortuitous, accidental? Is not that in itself significant?" The question is a natural one, for it is precisely during Earth evolution that the human being must develop intellect and reason—in other words, what is called the "normal" consciousness. At the end of Earth evolution, man should have reached the stage of perceiving law in those happenings and facts which today he considers accidental; they seem to him to be examples of pure "chance"; he can see in them no immediate evidence of the law manifested by happenings in nature; their conformity to law is wholly concealed. But precisely in those things which during Earth evolution conceal all evidence of law, seeming to be pure chance, man will learn to perceive a deeper conformity to law; when Earth evolution has run its course—but not until then—this law will present itself with the same inexorable "necessity" now associated with the laws of nature. If what are now called "chance" happenings appeared to be subject to the necessity of natural law, man would learn nothing from them. He would not be able to bring himself to say of some event: "I can either regard it as full of significance or as chance!" And so, because it is given into the hands of man and is a matter of his own free will whether he will apply intelligence and reason to what looks like "chance," he learns to find his way through earthly incarnations, to permeate with reason and intelligence what seems to be subject to no rule and to be brought merely by chance—so that what cannot, by its very nature, appear to him as evidence of rigid conformity to law appears, finally, as evidence of *spiritual* law.

We are able, here, to glimpse a very wise provision in world evolution, one which, if we grasp its significance, shows us that with extraordinary wisdom, certain things were ordained to appear as "chance." We ourselves must therefore unravel the threads of the law which must, first of all, be discovered within them. In order that for the sake of our own development, we might be taught self-knowledge and learn to weigh ourselves in the balance, it was left to our own will either to be wise or foolish, either to recognize conformity to law in so-called matters of chance, or to acknowledge only the inflexible laws of nature. As time goes on, it will be found that certain branches of science will refuse to apply anything but the abstract laws of outer nature and will insist upon labeling everything else "chance." These branches of science also, of course, represent activity in the life of soul, but if, as Goethe indicates at the end of *Faust*, man has turned his gaze to a higher world and has drawn nearer to what is spoken of by all true mysticism as the "Eternal Feminine," the realm in which the "Feminine" is the symbol for the eternal laws of nature and the sciences, if that has come to pass, these particular branches of science will, at the end of Earth existence, be regarded as the "Foolish

Virgins." On the other hand, spiritual science and what develops from it will be able to act in accordance with wisdom and law in those domains where the external sciences—the "Foolish Virgins"—are incapable of doing so. This will enable certain branches of science to be the "Wise Virgins" at the end of Earth evolution. And the beautiful parable in the Gospel indicates what will happen to the Wise and Foolish Virgins in due time (Matthew 25:1–13).

These things can lead us more deeply into the secrets of world evolution; and if we connect direct observation of the outer world with what we learn from spiritual science, a very remarkable factor comes to light. I will ask you now to accompany me in your thoughts.

You know that during the Earth period, more and more of the content, the knowledge, the achievements, the experiences of normal consciousness will become an integral part of man's being. But all evolution proceeds slowly and by degrees, and it will occasionally happen—indeed it sometimes happens now—that something which only in the future will be *normal* for man projects itself into the life of abstract reason and intellect, into the domain of the various branches of natural science; something not derived from the normal consciousness but connected with higher forms of consciousness projects itself into life. It is naturally veiled from the normal consciousness, but it points, nevertheless, to the deeper backgrounds of existence. Hence it is to be expected that whenever there is a projection of something which transcends the normal consciousness, it will also, strangely enough, be too striking to be lightly put down to "chance." In other words, as long as a person lives among his fellows with his normal consciousness only, he can speak lightly of "chance." As long as in mutual dealings among human beings there is no question of any element other than reason and intellect playing into their words and actions, so long will it be possible to speak glibly of "chance." For then, everything in their intercourse with one another and in external life which does not appear to be subject to law, will look so much like chance that it will be difficult to realize that even in what is, apparently, quite accidental, there *is* a connection regulated by law. But suppose something comes into our earthly life which cuts across the ordinary form of intercourse between human beings, based as it is merely upon intellect and reason—something which indicates a great deal more! So that you may see what I mean, I want to quote a special case which is to be regarded merely as an example but from which a great deal may be learnt if it is viewed in the light of spiritual science. It is an unpleasant, disagreeable case, but one from which we can learn, as in an experiment, what is actually at work.

In a certain place, it happened that a clergyman had alienated a woman's affection for her husband. He had had a kind of love affair with this woman, causing the husband deep grief. In the same place, there lived two men, friends of each other, who were devoted to the clergyman, not merely in their intellectual life but in their hearts and feelings. They were in his power, in the sense that his influence worked not only through the life of intellect and reason but also through the religious services and rites, through the element of spiritual life in religion. That the rites in this case had not produced any very good effect is not the point here; the point is the method adopted by the two men and the fact that the clergyman was their spiritual pastor. The two friends finally decided to do the clergyman a good turn and they consulted together as to how to get rid of the husband. The case has ugly features about it because the spiritual element is mingled with egoistic, human interests, bringing the whole thing near to the region of black magic. The two friends agreed to murder the husband, and actually did so. Thus they both incurred guilt, not merely by their intellectual decision but also because they had come under the sway of a psychological influence which affected the whole parish. We have therefore a curious case of human connections in which not only reason and intellect are operating but also something lying behind reason and intellect—because the clergyman, being what he was, was able to work with means connected with the spiritual life. What is to be expected, in the light of the principles of spiritual science known to us? Because events are causes and, as such, bring consequences, we can expect to find something else happening as a result of what then took place. In most occurrences connected merely with the operations of the reason and intellect, you will find many "chance" happenings, and you will speak of them lightheartedly as such, if you know nothing of spiritual science. But it will not be possible to speak of "chance" when there is definite evidence of a psychic influence having been involved in the causes of certain happenings. Here were two friends who had cooperated in the murder. In such a case, karma may be expected to work in a very definite way and all the circumstances oblige us to think of something more than "chance." Something very special must have been at work, for in this case there is evidence of an influence which might be termed "gray" or "black" magic. And what did, in fact, happen? The two murderers fell ill unaccountably, each with a different illness, and both died within the same hour. Those who insist upon speaking of "chance" will naturally want to do so here too; but those less determined to attribute everything to chance will try to reflect a little more deeply. What has been said in connection with this striking example will be confirmed in many ways if you are willing to probe thoroughly into incidents suggesting the interplay of something more than belongs specifically to the Earth mission and Earth consciousness; in this case, something rooted behind the sphere of external existence is in operation, indicating by the peculiar course of events, "abnormal" conditions—as common parlance would express it. But those who observe events from the standpoint of spiritual science will say: Here is a direct indication that because there is something different in the actual causes, the karmic course taken by the consequences of those causes will be strikingly significant.

Thus when we know of the power of the suprasensory behind the world of sense, the very way in which the external facts present themselves is an indication that such happenings differ from those in which there is no suggestion of any interplay of the suprasensory. Ordinary science would do well to investigate matters other than the pointless subjects which are dragged to light nowadays and which Friedrich Theodor Vischer[†]—in some respects a very shrewd writer—ridiculed in the following way. He said: There was once a learned scholar who went to Goethe's house and burrowed in all the dust that had been accumulating for years, examining every scrap of paper still lying in the wastepaper baskets; then he searched in all the corners, turned over the dirty rubbish heaps, and finally produced a treatise on "The Connection between Frau Geheimrat von Goethe's Frostbite and the

Symbolical Characters in the Second Part of *Faust*!" That is a rather radical example but in the catalogs of the most learned publications, similar things are to be found. It would be well if external science, instead of occupying itself with such matters as Vischer had in mind, were to turn to happenings like the one quoted, which provide striking evidence that occurrences attributed to "chance" but indicating the existence of psychical elements, clearly hint at *meaning*. The same thing applies, of course, to cases where no psychical factor is in evidence and which may therefore lightly be put down to "chance," only then it is not so easy to perceive the meaning, and spiritual observation is required to discern the presence of law. And so if we study life, in what confronts us as "chance," as an antithesis to law, we can see the clash of two worlds, literally the clash of two worlds. What do I mean by this?

Man has his Earth mission to fulfil—that is, he has to develop and elaborate what is now called "normal" consciousness. A wise world order has made it possible for many happenings to appear to him as chance; it therefore rests with his free will whether or not he will recognize in them the presence of law. But several currents, not only one, are always in operation. Everywhere there is an inflow of the spiritual, the spiritual of which man, too, is part. The spiritual would have been operating in an occurrence of the kind described above, even if the central figure had not been a clergyman; but in that case his own life of soul would not have been implicated to anything like the same extent.

This episode provides a clear illustration of the operation of another element, side by side with reason and intellect. Both elements play continually into life. Do not imagine for a moment that people who claim to be "monists," in other words, materialists, have emancipated themselves altogether from the spiritual, or that they "believe" in nothing at all, as they pretend. Monism is nothing but belief—belief, moreover, which obscures the spiritual. What is all important is to see through the illusion, the *maya*. Human prejudices being what they are, it is, of course, difficult always to see through *maya*; when people are deeply imbedded in *maya* it is by no means easy to see through it. Those who look at history today from the standpoint of materialism may say: "The course of evolution is such that on account of certain purely materialistic contrasts in the social life of man, some kind of collapse is inevitable, and out of this collapse a new order of society will grow." This is now being taken for granted in the domain of "historical materialism." It has been prophesied that the clash between classes and ranks will result in a collapse of the social order, and that a new order of society will arise from the ruins. A materialist who speaks in this sense will certainly be ready to admit that he believes in nothing but bases his judgment upon historical facts; and he will refer with a kind of inner satisfaction, even with glee, to "queer fellows" who spoke of an "Apocalypse," a "kingdom of a thousand years," a "millenium," of a different shaping of the future brought about by the spiritual worlds! He will look down upon them as eccentrics. But it never once enters his head that he is merely accepting another belief, substituting materialistic belief for belief in the spiritual. Those who are seekers after truth, however, must see through such things and emancipate themselves from *maya*.

Within us there is a clash of two worlds: one is connected merely with the operations of intellect and reason, resulting from the mission of the Earth as such; the other is connected with spiritual happenings which even in their apparent fortuitousness, speak an eloquent language (as in the instance given and in innumerable other cases).

What is it, then, that can help us, while adhering to the purpose and mission of Earth existence, to seek for the working of law in "chance," recognizing the wisdom with which world evolution has made it possible for certain things to appear as "chance," in order that when we ourselves become a little wiser, we shall wish to discover the operation of law in them? Without exonerating the weaknesses of the times, let us face the facts clearly.

With dauntless scientific daring, people of the present age place their reliance upon the laws of nature and are not afraid to bring the facts and happenings of nature into the framework of these laws. In this respect, people are truly courageous. And why? It may sound harsh but in a certain sense it is true to say that they are courageous because after that there is nothing more to do! No special courage is needed to recognize natural laws or to anticipate laws where external phenomena themselves speak so forcibly. In these days, as a matter of fact, there would be an inclination to pay greater respect to those who are bold enough to deny natural laws than to those who recognize them. If someone were to say: "People maintain that natural law exists, but after all, it, too, may well be only 'chance,'" this might evoke greater respect because it would be a radical and audacious step to admit the possibility of chance in the sphere of natural law. Nietzsche was one who came very near to the point of regarding everything as chance. Again, someone might say: "Even if hitherto the sun has risen every morning, that might likewise be a matter of chance; the daily sunrise may be regarded as chance as justifiably as other happenings." Such a statement might be forcible and audacious—but it would be false! In their recognition of natural laws operating in chemical and physical processes, people are undoubtedly courageous—the courage is certainly there, but it is cheap! The facts of nature do not readily lend themselves to being regarded as chance. Courage evaporates in the face of things generally designated as "chance"—just where it is most needed and when man ought to say to himself: "Although the happenings confronting me here seem to group themselves together quite haphazardly, I shall try to find a deeper meaning and purpose in them!" To see meaning and purpose in external chance means that the outer facts are being confronted with a strength of soul which also endures in the face of seemingly quite fortuitous happenings. The modern weavings of phantasy in regard to chance are the outcome of inner weakness, because people do not trust themselves to recognize law in the things which seem to be fortuitous. It is really cowardice on the part of science to accept the factor of chance and to be reluctant to introduce law into what presents itself as disordered chaos simply because law does not make itself immediately apparent. Hence the science of today which really lacks courage and is willing only to concern itself with natural laws, must be counteracted by the forcible and courageous science of the spirit which makes the soul strong enough to perceive law and order in apparently fortuitous happenings. This is the side of spiritual science which must make the human being strong enough not merely to recognize law where the external circumstances themselves compel him to be courageous, but where he must call upon all his inner forces and let them speak with the same compelling power with which nature happenings speak to him. Nature confronts the human being as a finished work. Within nature and by the side of nature, "chance" presents itself. Man himself is involved in this "chance" and much of what he calls his destiny is rooted in the laws underlying it. What is it, then, that is needed? We will now try to answer this question.

Something must take place of which the exoteric world has absolutely no idea. What is needed is an invigoration of the impulse which has led to the scientific method and attitude of today—an invigoration which cannot possibly be drawn from the domain of science alone. External science must receive an impulse deriving from spiritual research. For since external science allows itself to be coerced into accepting natural laws, it will be incapable of unfolding the courage that is necessary for the perception of spiritual law in the realm of the seemingly fortuitous. Spiritual science must constitute a new impulse which calls for the steeling of courage in human souls, an impulse which leads to something absolutely new in the world, even though this amounts merely to a new understanding of what has already been imparted to mankind but remains more or less unconscious; from our time onwards, people must become conscious of it. The need for a new impulse is everywhere apparent—even to those who resist it. They themselves realize the need quite clearly but they often proceed in a very strange way. They do not directly admit it, but lacking the courage to adopt the attitude of which we have spoken, they are willing, strangely enough, to be reconciled to all sorts of philosophical opinions concerning the spiritual world which make some slight compromise with the prevailing scientific mentality. Here and there, you will find that commendable "tolerance" is extended to teachings concerning a spiritual world, although it is not difficult to attribute this tolerance to likes and predilections which have a habit of persisting in sincere and scientifically minded people, but you may be quite sure that somewhere or other there will be exceptions. Those who think they have an unconditional right to judge, may say: "Yes, it is possible to come to terms with advocates of idealistic philosophy when they base their acceptance of a spiritual world upon reason." But when they hear about spiritual science or theosophy, these people adopt a curious attitude and act very strangely, for it makes them uneasy. They cannot altogether account for it, but one thing they know—namely, that they do not want to have anything to do with this kind of thing. On that point they are unyielding and then they are not quite so tolerant; they abuse spiritual science, say that it is fantastic and has no reasoned foundations. Even those who from superior heights occasionally extend tolerance to other forms of idealistic thought, adopt an attitude to spiritual science which almost confounds the saying of Goethe†: "The little fellows never notice the devil, even when he has them by the collar!" For theosophy seems to them to be the very embodiment of the devil. They do not usually say as much, but that is how things are.

There has lately been a striking example of this among our own ranks; attention may be drawn to it, for it is mentioned in the current German periodicals. For his doctorate at a northern university, one of our members submitted a thesis on "The Relation of the I to Thinking." If the man in question had been in the position in which I was lucky enough to be when I wrote my *Philosophy of Freedom*—which was before I was presenting under the name of "theosophy" the worldview I now represent—nobody would have any idea, any "false" idea, that this thesis on the relation of the I to thinking has any connection with theosophy; for there is absolutely nothing about theosophy in it, any more than there is in my *Philosophy of Freedom*, or in my *Truth and Science*. People had no inkling of what was behind these two works, and from time to time remarkably favorable opinions were expressed. I can give another example too. One day, because of my publications on Goethe, I was commissioned to write a chapter on Goethe's relation to natural science. The manuscript lay in the hands of the editor for a long time and the work did not appear. In those days it was practically a foregone conclusion that this particular section would have been trusted to me and not one of the persons concerned had any doubt about it. But you see, I had begun to use the word "theosophy," and I actually held an official position in the theosophical movement. The treatise was returned to me as "unusable." You can see what was going on behind the scenes then, and also in the present case. If our friend had not been a theosophist, nobody would have failed to recognize that here was a logical, dialectical thesis on "The Relation of the I to Thinking." But the university town where this episode took place is not very big. The writer was known to be a theosophist and so the professors had no use for his work. As the professors themselves happened also to be engaged in experimental psychology, their attitude was: We recognize law only where external compulsion holds sway. If anybody recognizes law where there is no external compulsion, as is the case in the relation of the I to thinking, his thesis is rejected as a matter of course! And so the thesis was turned down. But something else transpired. The thesis is written in a northern language with which very few people are conversant, and it was sent to an old German professor† who "by chance"—I say this advisedly—understands this language. He gave his verdict quite objectively and it was an extremely favorable one.

Another incident followed: I was recently sent an excerpt from the *Frankfurter Zeitung*† in which this matter was reported in such an incredible way that one no longer knew what it was about; for the matter was presented—although it really has nothing to do with theosophy—as though a debate about theosophy had taken place at a northern university! It was not about theosophy but about an entirely different point! And this should not be concealed. Namely, whether it is still possible to make an inroad against the intolerance of which we have spoken. The matter itself is actually never discussed. Other factors play into it, and thus you will find the most curious distortions about such events.

I mention these incidents—there are many others as well—so that you may know how things are and form your own judgments. Among theosophists, too, there are people who are ready to admit that here or there spiritual teaching is to be found, although they ought to realize that it is not a question of looking for a really new impulse "here or there" but in spiritual science itself. The impulses leading to progress in the world can only flourish when they are grasped in their full force. The human being, too, must lay hold of all the forces within him if he is to realize that apparent fortuity in the world is permeated with meaning and divine purpose. This is the impulse that must be given by spiritual science. Human beings must recognize that in the course of human evolution a point was once reached which must now be understood in a new sense, and in full consciousness. Significant allusion is made to it in the first chapter of the Gospel of Mark,† in the words: "The time is fulfilled and the Kingdom of Heaven is at hand; know yourselves, pay heed to the new message." And then, a few verses further on, a remarkable statement occurs concerning Christ Jesus.

In our movement, it is not a question of advocating orthodoxy or dogma but of indicating, in the evolutionary process of mankind, the coming of the impulse which leads to the strengthening of those inner forces whereby the human I attains self-knowledge, learning also to behold itself in the world and to draw into its own realm of law, what otherwise appears as "blind chance." Why is it that the phenomena of nature give no suggestion of chance? Why does man speak of *law* in the phenomena of nature? It is because after the Saturn, Sun, and Moon periods of evolution, the Spirits of Form, the Exusiai, intervened; and the manifested laws of nature are not abstract laws but, in a spiritual sense, the deeds of the Exusiai, of the Spirits of Form. When man observes the course of events in nature, he beholds, in the laws of nature, the deeds of the Exusiai. But his courage has failed. And where the Exusiai are not articulate, where they do not palpably indicate what they have laid into the facts and happenings of nature, man has no longer any inkling that there, too, the spiritual is at work as lawfulness. But he must strive to reach the stage where he speaks of those happenings which today he still ascribes to "chance," as the Exusiai speak in the facts of nature. Human courage has broken down. How does man speak of destiny, of destiny in humanity? He speaks just like the grammarians who have eyes only for the words and are not interested in the connections between the words, thinking, often enough, that there is no active, living power within them. Man must learn not only to see connective purpose in the facts of nature, in the deeds of the Exusiai, but out of an inner impulse, he must learn to speak of events in the life of humanity as though the Exusiai were being made manifest in what today seems to be pure chance. In order that this might be, there came one who spoke very differently from those who are ignorant of what lies behind apparently chance happenings. The one who came spoke not as the grammarians but as the Exusiai speak out of the facts of nature. Thus did Christ speak out of the mouth of Jesus! The Gospel indicates this in a wonderful way in that, to the abstract words, "And they were amazed at his teaching," it immediately adds: "For he taught as the Exusiai teach!" Where do the Exusiai teach? In the facts of nature! And with this same natural necessity, Christ spoke out of the mouth of Jesus concerning those realms of existence over which the laws of nature seem to exercise no sway.

Such is the impulse that must enter into human beings. Then, in the "chance" happenings of today, they will find the courage to recognize the kingdom of *spiritual law* and gradually to learn to speak of it as the Exusiai, the Spirits of Form, speak in the facts of nature.

The great Easter-impulse given to humanity consisted in this: There dwelt in Jesus of Nazareth the power of a being who spoke with the same inner necessity with which the laws of nature speak in the facts of nature, from the mineral kingdom of Earth, up and beyond the realm of the clouds, to the very realm of the stars. Thus did Christ speak in Jesus of Nazareth! And when man is able to fire his courage with this impulse, he will recognize conformity to law in all the facts of world existence, in the realm of nature and also in the realm of the spirit, where "chance" is thought to operate. There must come to humanity—free from all preconceived thoughts—a new understanding of where the might of the Christ-impulse lies, and of the heights to which the Christ-impulse can raise them.

With such thoughts we pass towards the festival held as a memorial that this impulse was vouchsafed to mankind. Much of what has been said in this lecture may well serve as a kind of Easter meditation, and you will then find that such thoughts can help to promote the true mood of soul in which to celebrate the festival, as this has also been characterized in our soul calender.

Lecture Four

BERLIN, APRIL 23, 1912

Before we turn to the subject of our study today, I must first draw your attention to the anthroposophical calendar which has just been published† and in which I have attempted to re-enliven what a calendar can be for the human being; for in this calendar, the cycles of time, the relationships of forces and cycles of time are led back to their origins, through which they can be recognized in occult imaginations. Much of what is expressed today only in the abstract symbols of the images of the zodiac can be enlivened if what was originally meant by the images of the zodiac is transformed into an imagination that can be felt. This has been done in the renewed zodiacal images rendered by the sensitive intuition of Fräulein von Eckhardtstein,† so that one can once again feel one's way into a living relationship with the heavens. You must only try to bring to life feelingly within yourselves what is given in the images.

You then find meditative formulas for the individual weeks of the year. These meditative formulas are particularly recommended for you because they contain that which can be brought to life in the soul and which then truly corresponds to a living relationship of soul forces to the forces of the macrocosm. What we could call the progress of time is directed and guided by spiritual beings, by spiritual beings who in their living mutual relationships actually determine time—one could even say, make time. Now, it is entirely abstract and merely allegorical when the human experience of time, the element of time in the human soul, is likened without further ado to processes that relate to time in the macrocosm. You will see that totally different experiences of the human soul, which in a certain sense have nothing to do with time, are given there. If you bring these things to life in your souls, then you will come to know the relationship that the soul can experience between the center and the periphery of sensory experiences. This peculiar relationship can be altered through these meditations. An imagination of the relationships of beings who determine the course of time can thereby be called forth, so that in these fifty-two formulas, one can, in fact, find the way from the microcosm to the macrocosm.

The calendar's outer form is only the exoteric side; for, in truth, we write 1879. The relationships of time that can be seen through occult observation should really be brought to expression here. This should have a starting point here, for, naturally, it is only a first beginning. With the Mystery of Golgotha, the birth of I-consciousness is given within humanity. And this fact will be increasingly understood in the spiritual culture of our earth as having significance for the whole future of humanity. Thus, one will gradually understand that it is justified to consider our current year to be 1879—that is, 1912 minus 33. This also means that time is calculated from Easter to Easter, that we do not begin with January, for if one sees in the birth of I-consciousness something essential for the spiritual evolution of humanity, it is also justified to be reminded every year of this fact by relating this birth of I-consciousness itself to the relationships between the microcosm and the macrocosm. A significant aspect of the relationship between microcosm and macrocosm is given when the Easter festival is thought of in connection with the birth of I-consciousness. The fact that today there is an attempt to set the date of Easter on a fixed day, rather than reading the date from the heavens, belongs quite naturally to the signature of our time, which, in regard to all external relationships, enters ever deeper into materialism and forgets what is connected with the spiritual. It will perhaps be necessary that over against industrialism, commercialism, and materialism in general, a remembrance is preserved in the anthroposophical stream, a remembrance of the concrete dates, which are not given through payment by cash or check but through the relationships of the universe. If the date of Easter is no longer set in accordance with the world of the stars, it will be the first great sign that the outer and inner culture, the completely materialistic and spiritualistic tracks, must go entirely side by side. One would stand before a hopeless prospect if one believed that from out of the materialistic culture a real ascent to spiritual facts is possible.

This is a first attempt for this year; I hope that the fact that anthroposophists use the calendar will support us in bringing it before the world in an ever more perfect form.

During the last few weeks, a number of friends from Germany have been with me on a visit to a field of theosophical work abroad—to Helsinki, in Finland. A visit of this kind to a far-off field of work always brings a realization of the unity of theosophical life all over the globe and also of its deep roots in the culture of the present day. It meant a great deal to me when our friends in Finland expressed the wish that I should speak to them about the venerable Finnish epic, the *Kalevala*.[†] As this wish was conveyed to me some time ago, I was able to occupy myself from the vantage-point of occultism with this remarkable poem of the Finns—who are themselves, in many respects, a unique people. And this brought to the fore once again, things of which I have spoken on other occasions, here and also elsewhere. A very definite experience comes to us when, independently of everything people have hitherto known concerning the spiritual worlds and have, in their own way, expressed in words, we ourselves strive for deeper insight into those worlds and man's relationship to them, and ask: How are we to understand what is contained in the many folk traditions that have been preserved through the centuries? How are we to apply to these recorded traditions the knowledge we have acquired concerning the suprasensory world? Although their language differs from that in which they have to be presented today, biblical and other records clearly based upon occult foundations are expressions, issuing from ancient times and from manifold periods of human evolution, of wisdom and knowledge which it is possible for us to rediscover today. These ancient records present a new aspect and seem to be imbued with a new power when we realize that in and from those same worlds to which we aspire along the path to spiritual knowledge and to initiation, great revelations have been given to the world in different epochs and in many ways.

We may well feel that the venerable Finnish epic, the *Kalevala*, has a special and unique occult significance. My own experience was very vivid and definite. This Finnish epic has been translated into every European language but it differs fundamentally and significantly from all other epic poems; no comparison with any of them is possible.

When my book *Theosophy* first appeared many years ago, independent observation of the spiritual world had led me to "member" the human soul into three: sentient soul, mind or intellectual soul, consciousness soul. Knowledge of the threefold soul was acquired purely through occult research and occult observation directed to the spiritual world quite independently of any tradition. Occult research was the only source consulted. And now, because our friends in the Finnish Section desired me to speak of the occult meaning of the *Kalevala*, it was necessary to make the poem the subject of spiritual investigation.

It has been emphasized repeatedly that human consciousness and the life of soul were not always as they are today. In primeval times of the evolution of mankind, our present mode of perception and thinking, our present relationship to the external world, simply did not exist; in those ancient times, the human being was endowed with a natural, innate clairvoyance. Turning our gaze to past epochs in the evolutionary process, we come to a period starting about the year 600 BC, when man's life of soul began to assume the form and character which were subsequently to lead to the much more abstract, scientific mode of thinking; before that time, vestiges and remains of the old clairvoyance, or memories of it at least, persisted among certain peoples for a very long time, among others for not so long. When we look back into the development of the peoples, we find in every case that consciousness as it is at present, developed only by very gradual stages. In very ancient times, normal human consciousness was imbued with a certain form of clairvoyance; and it was during the period of twilight denoting the disappearance of the old clairvoyance and the first beginnings of "modern" consciousness that the national epics, the folk epics came to birth.

It would, of course, have been absolutely impossible for people of primeval times to know anything about the threefoldness represented by sentient soul, mind soul, consciousness soul. But they possessed genuine clairvoyance, although it was dim and dream-like, lacking the light of intellect and reason in their present form. Before the dawning of the consciousness we know today, there were conditions, midway, as it were, between our waking and sleeping states, in which living memories arose of entirely different circumstances of life, when the relation of one human being to another was determined not by anything like consciousness as it is at present but by the old clairvoyance. And in their great folk epics the peoples depicted the experiences which arose within them during the period when the old clairvoyance was dying away and present-day consciousness was beginning to dawn.

The materialist says that man's life of soul has unfolded, by degrees, out of the material processes in the human organism—out of processes which are also to be found in lower forms of life. Spiritual science, however, makes it clear that the elements of "soul life" as they are in the animal would never have been able to give rise to the threefoldness of sentient soul, mind soul, consciousness soul, and that it is far more a matter of this inner trinity of the three "members" of the soul having flowed down from a spiritual world. Therefore when we look into the spiritual world we can speak of three down-flowing streams, with which three beings in the spiritual worlds are connected, beings who are the direct inspirers of the sentient soul, the mind soul and the consciousness soul. We have to think of the creators of these three manifestations of the life of soul in that suprasensory world with which, in primeval times, human beings were in direct communion.

We know that the moment our consciousness rises into the spiritual world, no matter whether this is the result of deliberate training, as will be the case today, or whether through the old clairvoyance, the human form becomes an "imagination." In those olden days, too, the soul attained to a form of imagination, beholding in pictures the outpouring of the threefold human soul from the spiritual world. The Finnish epic tells of three heroes. To begin with, these three beings seem strange and remarkable in the highest degree; they have something superhuman about them and at the same time something that graduates into the genuinely human. But if we examine the matter more closely and with occult means, it becomes apparent that these three figures, these three heroes, are the creators and inspirers of the threefold powers of the soul in man. The creator of the sentient soul is the figure to whom, in the *Kalevala*, the name of "Väinämöinen" is given; the creator of the mind soul is "Ilmarinen," and the creator of the consciousness soul, "Lemminkäinen." And so in the national epic of this remarkable people we find, in a form of imagination springing from the original, ancient clairvoyance, what is rediscovered by modern spiritual research. The human being of today has the outer form we see before us only because the foundations of this threefold life of soul were laid down in the course of evolution on Earth. I indicated this in the public lectures given in the Berlin Architektenhaus[†]: "The Origin of Man in the Light of Spiritual Science," on January 4, 1912; and "The Origin of the Animal World in the Light of Spiritual Science," on January 18, 1912.

We must picture to ourselves that there was a time in the process of the Earth's development when neither human beings nor animals were in existence, when all that was present was a kind of undifferentiated "substance"; the beings who first detached themselves were those which have reached the animal stage. When all the animals were there, man was still waiting until other conditions of Earth existence had set in, and because he had waited for these other conditions, he was able to become the recipient of his present form. In other words, while the animals developed their various forms on the Earth, man remained in the spiritual world above; his development began only when the animals had already assumed their destined forms. The foundations of the threefold soul—sentient soul, mind soul, consciousness soul—were laid in man and it was then possible for him to enter Earth existence in the external form in which he now lives.

With this in mind, we can say: Man, as the created being we know today, sent down the animal kingdom before him and then followed himself, when the Earth conditions were such that he could bring to manifestation in outer form, the threefold life of soul that had been laid into his being. What does this really mean? Knowledge of these occult truths restores to the traditions of religion, which rest upon occult foundations, their ancient value and meaning. Man received earthly substance into himself when he was able to recast, to remold it into his present form—a form able to receive the imprint of the threefold life of soul. Thus man elaborated earthly substance according to the laws of his life of soul, made earthly substance subject to the plan underlying his life of soul, and became the earthly man; he fashioned earthly substance after the model of the threefold, prototypal soul. Think of the biblical picture of the molding of the substance of Earth (not the "dust" but the *substance* of Earth) into man. We now discern profound meaning in this biblical conception upon which so much scorn has been poured by modern "enlightenment"—as it is called. For the passage points to the time when the animals, having descended at an earlier period, were already in existence and when, out of earthly substance, the being who now stands before us as bodily man, was fashioned, at a later stage, according to the model of the soul.

It is wonderful to find this process presented in the *Kalevala*, with great imaginative power, as the "forging" of a mysterious instrument called the "Sampo." The most curious explanations have been given of this mysterious instrument, the "Sampo." In reality, it is the human *etheric body*, forged by the interworking of the three soul members—it is the etheric body, the imprint of which is the physical body. All that is necessary here is to give indications, without entering more closely into details. The national epic of Finland quite obviously derives from the memory of the Finnish people in which clairvoyant perceptions of ancient times had been retained; through these perceptions, some knowledge still persisted of the descent of man as a being of soul—a threefold soul—into the physical body. What is noteworthy in such a matter is that in the old heroic sagas of humanity, we again find the truths and knowledge acquired today of the spiritual worlds. The *Kalevala* is an example of what is to be found in many ancient records of importance to humanity and is, moreover, one that emerged from oblivion only in the nineteenth century! For it had been entirely forgotten and was compiled during the course of that century from folk songs extant among the Finnish people.

In the early years of the nineteenth century, nothing had been written down of the *Kalevala* as we possess it today; the songs were heard from the people and had lived only among them. The simple fact is that in the nineteenth century a certain doctor realized that the people sang of many interesting things, and set about collecting the songs. Then a compilation was made and they assumed fresh importance. They attracted considerable attention and were translated into all the European languages. Scholars then proceeded to give senseless explanations of them, but all that really matters is that they are there, having lived among the people.

Approaching the matter with the spiritual knowledge we possess today, it becomes apparent, if we are willing to recognize it, that in what had survived there among the people and was gathered from among them, there is occult content which can be rediscovered today, just as occult content can be rediscovered in Homer's *Iliad*, in the *Odyssey*, in the *Niebelunglied*, and elsewhere. Only we must be willing to seek earnestly, not applying anything in the way of allegorical or symbolical interpretation, but rather allowing what is actually there to make its own impression upon us. What we ourselves have found in the realm of occultism shines forth in imaginations deriving from times of hoary antiquity. But in this case, there is something of particular interest, as I myself discovered. When the *Kalevala* came into my hands, I heard that the closing runes—which make allusion to a connection between the spiritual life of ancient Finland and Christianity—must obviously have been a later addition; for whereas all the rest bears the character of ancient paganism, the closing runes introduce an essentially Christian element—but very delicately and lightly. And then, strangely enough, I discovered that this belongs fundamentally to the *Kalevala*, that the poem is inconceivable without these closing runes. This means that in its origin and life among the people, the *Kalevala* quite naturally culminated in a delicate reference to Christianity—and, it may be added, to the most impersonal, "non-Palestinian" Christianity that it is possible to imagine, hardly recognizable by Christian concepts as they now are! Here, therefore, it is clear that from the same primeval soul, there issued something that could not have been born at the same time as Christian culture among the other peoples of Europe, for Christian culture arose long after clairvoyance had still been able to look back to those primeval ages when the threefold soul was "membered" into the human form. And so here, among the Finnish people, we have an indication of the link between the ancient clairvoyance and the influence subsequently brought into play by Christian culture. This is something quite remarkable and unique—perhaps nowhere else to be found on Earth. It may be that the veneration in which the *Kalevala* is held in Finland has preserved this epic from the fate that has befallen the *Iliad.* I do not know if many of you are aware that scholarship first of all hacked the *Iliad* into fragments and then declared that it was not written by a man bearing the name of "Homer"—indeed that it was not the work of a single writer but was only put together from collected songs, later on. The *Kalevala,* of course, was actually a compilation, but nevertheless, it forms a complete whole, one coherent whole. Possibly, in the future, a few changes here and there may be necessary, but nevertheless it is complete in itself. And so we have before us here, gathered from the consciousness of the people, a number of occult imaginations. If we follow the matter in the Akasha Chronicle, we find that the *Kalevala* leads back to the ancient and sacred mysteries of northern Europe, and that the truths it contains were inspired by the initiates, given forth to the people and instilled into them. Why have I been telling you these things?

Matters about which we have been hearing for years were also spoken of in Helsingfors and will be spoken of in other parts of Europe too. But the public lecture which I was able to give[†] on the subject of the occult content of the folk epics, with particular reference to the *Kalevala,* was something new, especially belonging to Finland. One then realized that the essence of spiritual science will more and more make itself felt over the whole Earth. For do we not all feel that with spiritual science we are at home in the spiritual life? We are everywhere at home, for spiritual science is the light which illumines the path to the spirit trodden by mankind all over the Earth. It is an overpowering experience to rediscover through spiritual science the real content of this collection of folk poems that form themselves into one whole. We find how right on into the ninth, tenth, and eleventh centuries, the folk soul became articulate in poetry, still possessing vital memories of the old clairvoyance once possessed by these unique

Finnish peoples who to this day retain many customs and arts reminiscent of an ancient form of magic. And then we realize that spiritual science alone can lead to an understanding of these things, make them intelligible to us!

One of the many signs of the great spiritual happenings of the near future may be indicated in the following way. Spiritual science has taken us into the region of an entirely unknown tongue—for the Finnish language differs from all other European languages; externally, one understands nothing of it and it is like being transported into an absolutely strange land. What knowledge does spiritual science bring us? How does spiritual science enable us to speak with this people who, so far as the last centuries are concerned, have remained remote from the other peoples of Europe? We speak with them about what is holiest and most sacred to them and is now coming to life again so strongly that people are reaching out for the *Kalevala* and the eyes of the whole world of culture are turning to it. In what is the most sacred possession of a people, we learn to understand the speech of the folk soul!

So, too, it can be the whole world over, when we realize what must be the very root-nerve of theosophical life. We are standing on the threshold of a new disclosure of spiritual truths. Attention has often been drawn to this, above all in my Rosicrucian mystery play, *The Portal of Initiation*.[†] Reference is there made to the fact that times are approaching when human souls will become more and more open to receive revelations from the spiritual world which will break in upon them as a kind of natural experience. In the course of the next three thousand years, people will gradually "grow into" the spiritual world. Through spiritual science, however, we must learn to understand why, and to what extent this will come about.

In the first, very ancient period of the post-Atlantean era, that of the Holy Rishis of India, culture "flowed," as it were, directly from and was inspired by the human etheric body; in the epoch of ancient Persia, culture was inspired by the sentient body, the astral body; in the Egypto-Chaldean epoch by the sentient soul; in the Greco-Latin period by the mind or intellectual soul; and in our own epoch by the consciousness soul. There will follow a form of culture inspired by the spirit self, and so on. If you keep in your minds a picture of the whole course of post-Atlantean culture, you will find, as it were, a descending curve until the time of the Greco-Latin epoch. It is clearly perceptible, and permits of no denial, that this age represents the lowest point of man's descent to the physical plane; the most characteristic and remarkable feature of the fourth post-Atlantean epoch is that spiritual life is all interwoven, intertwined, entangled with life on the physical plane. But in that same epoch comes the impulse of the Mystery of Golgotha—and necessarily so. You have only to think of what you already know in this connection. There is, however, something else of importance to remember. The actual course of human evolution comes to expression in manifold ways in the life of the *individual.* In the little book, *The Education of the Child in the Light of Spiritual Science,*[†] it is said that up to the seventh year, the development of the physical body is of primary importance: this phase corresponds, in the evolutionary process of mankind as a whole, to the period *preceding* the Atlantean catastrophe. The period of life between the seventh and the fourteenth years is a recapitulation—although veiled and obscured—of the culture connected with the etheric body, which reached its highest glory in the epoch of ancient India. The period from the fourteenth to the twenty-first year of life is a recapitulation of the culture inspired by the astral body, corresponding to the epoch of ancient Persia. The Egypto-Chaldean period is reflected in the life of the individual human being from the twenty-first to the twenty-eighth year; and the Greco-Latin epoch is reflected in the life of the individual between the twenty-eighth and thirty-fifth years. This is a very important period; for just as at that time post-Atlantean humanity swung over from a descending to an ascending culture, so there can be a turning-point in the life of the individual between the twenty-eighth and thirty-fifth years. At the middle point of his earthly existence, the individual faces at one and the same time a descending and an ascending curve of life. After the thirty-fifth year, he passes, as it were, into the period of outward decline, into a process of "withering." In the individual human life at this time there must be something which corresponds with the swing-over from the descending to the ascending curve of culture. That the Mystery of Golgotha took place during this particular period of the life of Christ Jesus, between the twenty-eighth and thirty-fifth years, was not a matter of chance; it could not be otherwise, as those who know anything of these connections will realize. The Mystery of Golgotha could only be enacted during the period of life connected specifically with the development of the mind soul. Since the end of the Middle Ages, we have passed into the period of the unfolding of the consciousness soul. This will last for a very long time; and then will come the period of the evolution of spirit self.

Now in the life of the individual there is something irregular—magnificently irregular—about the appearance or awakening of the I. At some future time I will elaborate this, but at the moment I can only indicate it. The regular course of things is the development of the physical body up to the seventh year, of the etheric body up to the fourteenth year, and so on, up to the twenty-eighth year. Then, and only then—if conditions took a regular, straight-forward course—would the I awaken in the mind soul; for only then does the external organization of the human being contain the proper and suitable instrument for the I. But the I awakens, actually, at a very early period of childhood, quite independently of the external organization—at that point of time to which, in later life, the memory reaches back. Why is it that the birth of the I, instead of occurring between the twenty-eighth and thirty-fifth years, in accordance with the development of man's external organization, actually occurs during the earliest years of childhood? It is because the luciferic forces have brought about a certain displacement as between the inner and the outer man. The luciferic forces are connected with "retardation" in time. The I within us is grounded upon luciferic forces, upon remembrance of what has remained to us of our experiences in life. Lucifer emancipates the I which is thus made free and independent of the outer organization. For a time, it was necessary for man to be connected, externally, with something other than his I alone. To maintain his rightful place, it was necessary to form a link with a being who had lived during the fourth post-Atlantean epoch, had reached his thirtieth year, and was then inspired by the Christ, by a power which could not live on the Earth beyond the thirty-third year, but which in the thirty-third year passed through death. To begin with, it was an external, historical link. What I have often described to you from the one side, I want you now to consider from the inner side. The human being remembers back to the point in his life when consciousness awakens; his remembrance stretches back to the birth of the I: for his actual entrance into Earth existence is shrouded in sleep. Of what precedes the birth of the I we have to be told by our parents, by our elder brothers and sisters, by our seniors. Just as the memory of the human being now reaches back to the awakening of this I—the luciferic I—so, later on, he will see, as in an imagination, another I, another I before him. This will come about during the next three thousand years as a development of great significance in the evolution of humanity. In the future, man will remember that at a certain point of time in his childhood, the luciferic I awakened; and he will also remember back to another point of time, when the Christ-I appears, in contrast to the luciferic I. Instead of the one point, there will be two. The fact that this will arise as a memory will be the proof that the Christ-event has not still to take place, but that it has already taken place. In short, just as a person at the present time remembers back to the awakening of the I, so, in time to come, the imagination of the second I will be within his field of remembrance, enabling him to find the way to what we describe as the new appearance or manifestation of Christ.

The fact that man is growing onwards to new experiences, spiritual experiences of an entirely new kind, is something that must be understood in the light of spiritual science; for naturally, there must be preparation for these experiences. The human soul is moving towards new experiences. That is one thing that must be realized in spiritual science. The second is this. These new experiences are of such a nature that they will bring peace, concord, and harmony upon the Earth and among men. And it will indeed be so! That is why it is such an overpowering experience to be able to understand the folk spirit in another corner of the Earth. The poetry inspired by the folk spirit is illumined by spiritual science—but we must be willing to steep ourselves in what actually springs from this folk spirit, and interpolate nothing else. That must be the attitude of a spiritual conception of the world.

And now let us face facts. What is the present position? People have quarreled, have fought and shed blood through the ages over religious opinions; but if the root-nerve of spiritual science is understood, there will be no more conflict in the future about particular religious opinions. People's minds will be directed to the spiritual facts themselves, and differences of opinion on the various problems of religion will exist just as they exist in other spheres—but not in such a way as to lead to bloodshed and strife; for it will be recognized that the revelations given to the different peoples point back to vast and mighty wisdom. Men will find the foundation and ground of this wisdom and recognize the truths that are contained in the various religions. The science of comparative religion has done far-reaching work in connection with the several religions and the points of resemblance to be found in them. Splendid results have been achieved—but what, in reality, is the attitude that is almost invariably adopted? The attitude, more or less clearly expressed, is that all the religions are false! The science of comparative religion brings out the errors far more clearly than the truths contained in the religions. Spiritual science, on the other hand, directs its attention to the truths, to the initiation knowledge which they contain. To what does this lead? What, for instance, will be the attitude of a Christian to a Buddhist? The Christian will realize the sublimity and splendor of the Buddhist system; because Christianity itself will learn to understand reincarnation and karma, the Christian will recognize the greatness of this teaching of Buddhism. And he will have knowledge, too, of the existence of certain individualities in world evolution who rise from the rank of "Bodhisattva" to that of "Buddha." The Christian will understand something which spiritual development alone can make clear to him—namely, that in the twenty-ninth year of his life, the son of King Suddhodana became the Buddha. The event could only take place at that particular age, as a study of spiritual science will show. These things are connected with what is said in the little book *The Education of the Child*. With this knowledge, the Christian will also realize that such a being does not descend again to Earth in a physical body. Christians who are theosophists, or, if you prefer, theosophists who are Christians, do not regard these teachings of Buddhism as mythical fables, but, together with the Buddhists, believe in the truth that in his twenty-ninth year the Bodhisattva became Buddha and will not return in a physical body. The Christian respects this belief; he believes what the Buddhist believes, is at home on the soil of Buddhism, does not regard it as childish phantasy. He knows that in the royal son of King Suddhodana there dwelt an individuality who rose to such spiritual heights that he need never again descend into a physical body but sends his influence in another way into the evolution of humanity. Understanding the truths contained in Buddhism, the Christian will never interfere in the spiritual life of a Buddhist in such a way as to alienate him from his religion.

And what will be the attitude to Christianity of a Buddhist who also happens to be a theosophist? He will try to grasp what it signified when in a man known as Jesus of Nazareth, in the thirtieth year of his life, the I was replaced by the being whom the fourth post-Atlantean epoch of culture called the "Christ," and who dwelt for three years in the body of Jesus of Nazareth. He will understand what is meant by saying that the "substance" of Christ, which passed through death with Christ Jesus, has streamed over human culture; and he will try to understand that this life, from the Baptism by John in the Jordan to the Mystery of Golgotha, represents an event which took place once and once only in the evolution of mankind, and that like the Buddha, he who was once incarnate in Jesus of Nazareth can never again come down to the Earth. The Christian who is also a theosophist understands that the Bodhisattva, having become Buddha, ascends into the spiritual worlds; the Buddhist who is also a theosophist recognizes those spiritual facts which form the essence of Christian belief—namely, that the Christ-being descended into the body of Jesus of Nazareth, lived in that body for three years and passed through death; and that thereafter his power streams through the spiritual atmosphere of the Earth. Mutual understanding among the confessions of faith on the Earth and therewith mutual harmony—that is the essence and core of theosophical teaching. If the Christians were to say that an individuality might appear as the reincarnated Buddha, it would be an absurdity, and the Buddhist peoples would rightly resist any such teaching being disseminated among them. Discord would inevitably arise in communities of Christians if they were informed that the Christ might incarnate again in the flesh. The task of theosophy is to bring about mutual understanding between the religions on Earth which are founded upon initiation. When this is understood, theosophy will live truly in the hearts of men; there will be no founding of new sects, no proclamations of new, physical prophets, for whom humanity no longer waits in that external sense. People will then learn to understand the Rosicrucian principle which has remained unbroken since the founding of Rosicrucianism—namely, that those who are charged with the task of teaching may not previously speak to the outer world of their mission. Indeed it is a venerable rule in Rosicrucianism that a teacher of the Rosicrucian way is never outwardly proclaimed as such by his contemporaries; the fact that he *is* such a teacher may not be spoken of until a hundred years after his death—not before—because only so can the *impersonal* element be preserved in a genuine spiritual movement.

Clear understanding of the fact that we are entering upon a phase of development in which the human soul will become more and more aware of the inflow of the spiritual and thus of the suprasensory Christ-event of which we may speak prophetically—and a clear realization that theosophy must always lead to an understanding of what is sacred and holy to each individual—these are the two factors which make one a true theosophist within the theosophical movement. Indeed, a person's very attitude to them can tell us whether he has or has not understood the task of theosophy in the present age.

Lecture Five

BERLIN, MAY 2, 1912

WHEN WE THINK of all the achievements of the spiritual life, all the insight into the spiritual world and conceptions of the universe which have come to birth during the course of human existence, we have, on the one side, a picture of great and significant progress in the evolution of mankind on Earth; and when this progress is investigated by spiritual science, it becomes clear that the human being—the single individual—participates in this general progress in that he passes through the successive epochs and time periods in reincarnations; in this way he is able not only to preserve everything that his soul has assimilated in ancient and more recent times, but also to play a real part in the whole evolutionary process. Thus when a person has lived as a being of body and soul in one epoch of culture, he does not vanish from the field of evolution but remains, in order again to take part in what Earth existence has later become. In a general sense, progress of this kind is certainly to be perceived. But many of our studies will remind us that this progress is not so straightforward a matter that it could be said to begin with the simple and the primitive, rising from thence into the heights; on the contrary, it will be found that progress—indeed, the whole process of evolution—is full of complication.

The first post-Atlantean epoch of culture after the great Atlantean catastrophe was that of ancient India. Its sublimity and power of vision into the spiritual worlds have never since been equaled, nor will its heights be reattained until the seventh post-Atlantean epoch—after the fifth and sixth have run their course. Thus, in certain forms of spiritual life there is a decline, followed again, in due course, by an ascent. Greco-Latin culture, for instance, was a most noble expression of the inner union existing between the Greeks and their art, and of the wise ordering of civic life in Greece and Rome, whereby a certain harmony in the conditions of life on the physical plane was created. But an utterance of a great Greek is also indicative of the character of this epoch: "Better it is to be a beggar in the Upper World than a king in the realm of the Shades.[†]" This indicates that in an epoch of golden prime on the physical plane, men had only very limited consciousness of the significance of the spiritual world lying behind and beyond the physical plane. Since that time, the intensity of the union between the human being and life on the physical plane has waned, together with the noblest fruits of that union; on the other hand, however, mankind begins gradually to ascend once again to the spiritual worlds. This will serve as an illustration of the complicated course taken by human evolution. When emphasis is laid on the blessings and light-filled aspects of one particular epoch, this most certainly does not imply that lesser value is to be attached to other epochs which lack certain characteristics. Although we speak again and again of all that Christianity has brought into the world, we know that its impulse is only beginning and that the spiritual heights attained in the East before the coming of Christianity have not again been reached. All this must be remembered, because there must be no thought or suggestion that in bringing forward the merits of one epoch, we do less than justice to the greatness and significance of others. In this sense, I ask you to pay attention to a difference that is neither a merit, on the one side, nor a failing, on the other: I want simply to describe a certain difference between pre-Christian, oriental culture and Christianity (not pagan or even ancient Hebrew culture)—a difference which becomes clear when insight into Christianity has been deepened by spiritual science.

When we look into the oriental worldview, we find a firmly established principle to which repeated allusions are made but to which, up to now, Christianity has paid little heed. The oriental worldview has knowledge of the great cosmic laws revealed today by spiritual science—namely, those of the *return of the human being in different Earth lives*, and of *the law of karma*. Whereas Christianity through the centuries has had eyes only for the life of a man between birth and death, and its continuance in a simple heavenly life, the oriental world possesses definite knowledge of the return of man in repeated lives on Earth; and the knowledge of this great manifestation of law in the evolution of humanity constitutes much of the profound significance in oriental worldviews. As a result of this, oriental teaching contains something regarding the leaders and great heroes of human evolution which differs fundamentally from anything taught in the West. In oriental worldviews, we find references to beings of whom it is said from the outset that they return again and again and that the importance of their influence can be measured by their achievements in successive Earth lives. The very name "Gautama Buddha" is indicative, for "Buddha" is not a proper name like "Socrates" or "Raphael," but denotes a rank. The world of thought from which Buddhism has grown speaks of many Buddhas. "Buddha" is a rank. Before "Gautama Buddha," the royal son of King Suddhodana, became the "Buddha" of whom oriental teachings speak, he was a "Bodhisattva." In other words, the oriental worldview perceives the individuality who passes through the different incarnations, ascending from incarnation to incarnation and finally reaching the height at which the rank of "Buddha" is attained. Such an individuality is then no longer called by a proper name. In speaking of the characteristics of the Buddha, Buddhism rarely refers to "Prince Siddhartha," but far more often to a rank, attained not only by him but to which every human being can attain. And so, in pointing to the great leaders, the East points to the individuality who passes through repeated Earth lives; the greatness and significance of these leaders are attributed to the merits they acquired through repeated lives on Earth.

And now compare this with characteristic features of Western culture. There we are told of the greatness of a Plato, a Socrates, of a figure like Paul; even in the Old Testament, a figure like Moses stands out in strong relief, and, later on, Raphael, Michelangelo, Leonardo da Vinci among many others. The West speaks of the *single personality*—not the "individuality" who passes through repeated lives on Earth. Attention is directed not to the being who goes on from birth to birth, from death to death, but to the one personality who lived from a certain point of time to another. The East directs its attention more to the onward progress of the individuality from one incarnation to another, whereas Western culture has been little concerned as to who Socrates, for example, could have been in previous Earth lives, or what becomes of him in later lives. It is the same with Paul and with all the others. This is a very fundamental difference. The matter may be summed up by saying that the whole trend of the West hitherto has been to lay emphasis upon the importance of the personality, of the single life of the human being. Only now, when we are on the threshold of a great change in the spiritual life, are we beginning—having acquired in Western culture a gauge as it were for the single personality—to discern a principle of existence which oriental culture accepts as a matter of course—namely, the development of the individuality within the single personalities, through many lives. A perspective of the future fraught with great significance is here opened up, of which mankind will stand increasingly in need.

Christian thought has actually lost sight of something which the East has always possessed and knowledge of which has now to be reacquired. The course of evolution is such that certain outworn fragments must be discarded and new elements added; ancient heritages must be rescued again, but in a new form and through a new impulse. In olden times, clairvoyance was a natural gift in humanity. It had to fade away and be replaced by thinking based upon purely external observation and perception; this will be enriched by the clairvoyance of the future and will add something of untold significance to human life. The West had to pass through a period during which mankind was split up, as it were, into separate personalities, but now that human beings stand on the threshold of a deepening of thought and experience, they will themselves be aware of a longing to find the thread uniting the fragments which make their appearance in the life of the human being between birth and death. The light of understanding will thus be shed on the forces which flow onwards through the stream of spiritual development and human progress. Let us illustrate this by a particular example:

In the lecture on "The Prophet Elijah in the Light of Spiritual Science"[†] I spoke of what occult research reveals concerning this prophet. I do not propose to go into further details now but will only say that in the light of occult knowledge, Elijah was one who proclaimed with power and deep intensity that the primal, original form of what humanity may call the "divine" can be glimpsed only in the innermost core of man's being, in the I. The great prophetic message of Elijah proclaimed that everything the outer world can teach is, at most, semblance and parable, that realization of the essential nature of man can only arise in the I. Elijah could not, in his time, proclaim the power and significance of the single, human I, but he proclaimed the existence, as it were, of a divine I, external to the human being. Men must recognize this divine I, must realize that it rays into the human I. That this divine I rises up within the human I and there unfolds its full power—such is the knowledge won by Christianity. The work and mission of Elijah are therefore a true heralding of Christianity. This can be said when the life of Elijah and his place in the history of human evolution are being described in the light of occult knowledge.

And then we may think of another life, the life of the personality known as John the Baptist. From the mouth of John, humanity was to learn what the immediate future held in store: "Change the attitude of your souls! Do not look back to the times that are past, when men sought to find the divine only at the starting-point of evolution; look, rather, into your own souls and into the deepest core of your being and then you will know that the Kingdoms of Heaven are near." This was the substance of the message of the Baptist. In other words: the phase of development has come when, in very truth, the I can find the divine *within itself.* The form in which Christianity was heralded by Elijah has changed with the flow of time. Something altogether different is represented by John the Baptist. But through spiritual science and a deepened understanding, we realize that one and the same being lived in the prophet Elijah and in John the Baptist. We add to our understanding of the single life a principle of knowledge already possessed by the East, only the East did not lay such emphasis upon the power and force inhering in the single personality.

Going further, we can speak of that most remarkable personality who lived from 1483 to 1521, was born on a Good Friday and through this very fact indicated, as it were, his living connection with the Mystery of Golgotha. I am referring, of course, to Raphael, the great painter. In the Western world, as is only to be expected, it is customary to study Raphael as a figure in himself, but it will very soon become clear to deeper insight that what the West has to say with regard to Raphael has many shortcomings. This figure of Raphael presents a remarkable spectacle to those who aspire for a more profound understanding. It is as though his genius came with him at birth. In a manner of speaking, it can be said that he "let himself be born" on a Good Friday, in order to indicate his connection with the Mystery of Golgotha. It is quite obvious that from the very first, his life gave promise of all his subsequent greatness. Orphaned at an early age, he was thrown out into the world and finally into the brilliance and splendor of Rome; there, within the span of a short life, we see him rise step by step to heights of fame. What is there to be said about this remarkable life? Think of the environment into which Raphael was born—it was in the period at the turn of the fifteenth and sixteenth centuries. It was a time when disputes in the world of religion were rampant and widespread, when Christianity was scattered into countless sects over the whole Earth, when mighty and also terrible conflicts were being waged in Christendom. And now we turn to Raphael's paintings. It is a strange experience! They seem to make us forget what was happening all around in the Christian world at the time, and a kind of jubilation at the power with which Christianity has taken root in human evolution streams out from them. Think of a picture like *The School of Athens*, as it is generally called. We see all those remarkable figures, deciphered by pedants with the aid of historical guide-books, as Socrates, Diogenes, and so forth. This, however, means nothing whatever from the point of view of art. But if we take the New Testament and read the Acts of the Apostles attentively, we feel that in this picture we have before our very eyes the whole vivid difference between the pre-Christian views prevailing in Greece and those of Christianity; we also find this in the picture usually, though erroneously, known as the *Disputa*. *The School of Athens* really depicts the scene in the New Testament when Paul came among the Greeks, saying to them: "Until this day you have heard of many gods; but the divine does not express itself in images. You have spoken great words concerning the living gods, but there is something still greater: the glory of the God who died on the cross and has risen again!" We feel the power of the message as we stand before the picture called "The School of Athens," and look at the remarkable figures of the philosophers listening attentively as Paul speaks. When the picture is actually before us, the pedantic interpretation given to it later on—that the central figures are Aristotle, Plato, and so forth—fades into insignificance. We feel that Raphael was trying to depict the moment when Paul came among the Greeks. If we study the New Testament closely, we shall be able to identify the figure of the man with the hand pointing forward so significantly, as a personality drawn from the New Testament account. The New Testament, therefore, provided the model for a personality depicted in this picture—namely, the personality of Paul.

And so we pass from one picture to another, forgetting all the statements that have been made about the one or the other, for a great force streams out of them; we feel that Christianity is living on in its mightiest power in the paintings of Raphael and that they portray a Christianity in which there can be no strife or splitting into sects. Recent times, however, have had little understanding of the Christianity which pours its living influence through Raphael's paintings. When we look at them even more closely, still another feeling comes to us. It is as though their creator wanted to portray the eternal youthfulness, the eternal power of victory in Christianity. And then perhaps we ask ourselves: In what form did the influence of these paintings live on?

Before very long, a despot like Bernini[†]—who accomplished so much for art—was giving warning against imitation of Raphael; it is even possible to say that Raphael was "forgotten." In Germany and in the west of Europe during the eighteenth century there is a strange story to tell in regard to people's understanding of Raphael. In the whole of Voltaire's works,[†] you will find hardly a mention of Raphael. The name of someone else may also occur to you, although he held a very different view later on. Goethe's experience when he visited the Dresden Gallery for the first time was a strange one. When you yourselves stand before the *Sistine Madonna*, you will probably imagine that the picture must have filled Goethe with enchantment, and this may well be assumed in view of all the hymns with which he later sang its praises. We have to remember, however, what he had heard from the officials of the Dresden Gallery and from those who were the official custodians of the picture. He was informed by them that the child in the arms of the mother, the child whose eyes express a rare gift of seership, was painted with realistic vulgarity, that it could not be from the hand of Raphael himself but must have been painted over by someone else; and that the little heads of angels could not possibly have been Raphael's own work. The coming of the Sistine Madonna to Dresden was not crowned with triumph! But at any rate it is to Goethe's credit that after he had learnt to appreciate Raphael, he contributed a great deal towards an understanding of the Sistine Madonna and of Raphael himself.

Now let us think of the course taken by evolution in the nineteenth century, leaving aside what occurred in Catholic countries and turning our attention to Protestant lands in which the dogma concerning the Virgin Mary is not essential to faith. There, not only the *Sistine Madonna* but all the other Madonnas of Raphael are veritably crowned with glory! Without thinking now of the originals, the many excellent engravings and reproductions are a proof of how people have endeavored to present Raphael's creations to the world in the most perfect form possible. Few people, after all, have the opportunity of seeing the originals themselves. Naturally, no reproduction can convey the essence of the artistic power in a picture; to suppose any such thing would be ignorant and barbaric. But something else made its way into the evolution of mankind: in regions which would have nothing to do with the dogma of the Immaculate Conception, a form of Christianity independent of all differences of doctrine found entrance. While men have fought for these differences of doctrine in theories and systems, a picture of this great mystery—in the characters of an occult script, as it might be said—found entry in the reproductions of Raphael's art, filling the mystery with new life. Here again is a heralding of Christianity from which great and glorious fruits will ripen in the future. And understanding of these things will be quickened by the experiences which have arisen in human beings at the sight of the *Sistine Madonna*, the *Madonna del Pesce* and other Madonnas, or from *The School of Athens*, the *Disputa*, and other paintings of Raphael. Without being aware of it, people have in their souls today the feeling of an inter-denominational Christianity, conveyed by this wonderful occult script.

Raphael both heralded and established a new impulse in Christianity, although, to begin with, he was not understood. Occult investigation finds that the same individuality who once worked in Elijah and later in John the Baptist lived again on earth in Raphael. This helps us to understand how the forces develop in the same soul from life to life and to discern the effects of earlier causes. The Baptist was beheaded; his work came to light again in the achievements of his great successor. The new proclamation of the Baptist in the Raphael life was for long ages forgotten. It came to life again in what spiritual science teaches concerning the Christ-impulse. What a light shines in our understanding when we gather up the threads leading through the single personalities, and in what vivid perspective the single personality stands there before us!

I said that the paintings of Raphael are like chants of jubilation at the might of Christianity. Raphael naturally keeps to the accepted events and facts, but out of his feelings he is able to portray them with a unique power. As our eyes wander over his paintings, we realize with what majesty and sublimity he portrayed the forces of Christianity, and we ask ourselves: What is it that Raphael did *not* paint? He painted no scene on the Mount of Olives, no Crucifixion. True, he painted Christ carrying the cross, but it was a very poor picture and gives the impression of having been done to order. Neither did he paint any of the scenes leading directly to the Crucifixion. His creative genius begins to reveal itself again only when he portrays the figure of the great successor of John—the figure of Paul in *The School of Athens*; or when, passing over the other events in the life of Christ, he paints *The Transfiguration*. What Raphael has *not* painted helps us to understand that it was alien to him to portray those events on Earth (not events in the spiritual world) which took place after he was beheaded in his previous life. We realize why it was that Raphael painted fewer pictures of these particular events. When we look at the pictures, we feel that all those which portray events subsequent to the beheading of John the Baptist, are not, like the others, born of earlier remembrances.

As we think of all this, another feeling, too, may arise in us. In a few more hundred years, what will have become of all the paintings which have been such great and mighty symbols in mankind? True, for some time yet the reproductions will be left to us, but not the originals—for so very long. Anyone who looks today with sorrow in his heart at Leonardo da Vinci's *Last Supper* realizes what will become of the physical materials used in these pictures. It dawns upon us, too, that they can only be truly appreciated when, through spiritual science, we understand what it is that Raphael has painted, for example, in *The School of Athens* or the *Disputa*. What is to be seen today on the walls of the Vatican in Rome has been ruined by the many restorations. No real idea of the originals is possible, for they have been so grievously spoilt by the restorations. What, then, will have happened in another few centuries? No means of preservation devised by the mind of man will be able to prevent the materials from deteriorating. In another few centuries, everything will have vanished. The subjects themselves, of course, will still be known; but the creations of Raphael's own hand will disappear. And then the thought arises: Is the process of human evolution such that things continually come into being only to sink, finally, into non-existence?

Our gaze wanders further and falls upon the youthful figure of a German poet—Novalis.[†] To begin with, we find in his writings a most wonderful and unique resurrection of the Christ-idea, of which the following may be said. If we steep ourselves in spiritual science and, with the means it provides, try to understand the coming of the Christ-impulse into the evolution of humanity, and then turn to Novalis—wherever we look, something seems to spring into life. Inspirations of the greatest grandeur concerning matters of spiritual science are to be found everywhere. Inspirations that are like lofty dreams of science. From Novalis comes something that finds its way into mankind like a seed—a seed which will spring to life in times to come. Here again is a heralding of Christianity! In spite of all differences, it is again a beginning, just as the work of the Baptist was a beginning. We are drawn irresistibly to the remarkable figure of Novalis, feeling that a stream of living theosophy goes out from him, inspired by the power of Christianity. We feel that here, too, is a proclamation of Christianity for the future.

Occult investigation finds that in Elijah, in John the Baptist, in Raphael, in Novalis, the same individuality lived and worked. In Raphael there is a new resurrection of the work of John the Baptist, and it may indeed be said: Raphael himself is able to ensure that his work will not perish when his paintings are no longer to be seen on the walls, just as he was able to prevent other achievements from passing away. Just as he provided for the revival, in a new form, of what it had once been his mission to proclaim, so will he always provide in incarnations yet to come. Thus does the individuality bear through eternity what has once been accomplished.

It may be that concrete examples like these, given as illustrations of abstract laws and principles, will do more than the external teachings of spiritual science to render the theosophical conception of human life as intelligible as those things which confront us in the outside world. Deep insight may come to us when, in the light of such concrete examples, we observe processes operating more secretly in the evolution of the human soul. As spiritual research is still a young science, people who have studied Raphael hitherto can naturally know nothing of the power and impulse he bears through the ages. But because the time has come when the idea of the reincarnation of the human being is to dawn, even though nothing concrete is known about it, undefined intuitive feelings may arise here and there. A striking example of this has come again to my mind during the last fortnight. I remembered how Herman Grimm,[†] a most gifted writer on the history of art and a distinguished student of Raphael, speaks of the painter. Naturally, when Herman Grimm was writing about Raphael, he knew nothing of spiritual science and studied only the single life of Raphael. He observed Raphael's fame through the centuries, its decline and subsequent growth, and discerned how, in his creations, Raphael lives on through time. And then there dawned upon Herman Grimm the remarkable thought which he expressed in his work on Raphael (he had wanted to write a volume, but it remained a mere fragment). He says there, expressing an entirely instinctive feeling: When we ponder on the things that will endure in the evolution of mankind, and thus catch a vista of the future, the thought arises that all these things will be lived through again! This is an eloquent indication of how the thought of "re-experience" rises instinctively, like a longing, in the souls of men who observe evolution thoughtfully and sensitively, for the very reason that without such a conception, the rest has no meaning. This is of infinite significance. And when we reflect on these things, an idea that is beautiful and true comes to us of what spiritual science will be able to do for the evolution of humanity, and of the enrichment which human life in all its forms will receive through knowledge of the laws on reincarnation and karma. But if the life of humanity is to be thus enriched, human beings will have to learn to observe the spiritual with the same exactitude with which they observe the physical; they will have to perceive how repetition in the physical world is a great law of existence, and that recurrence—as in the return of the soul into the body—is also a law governing the return of the fruits of the various lives. Such an experience, however, is always preceded by others—by human longings and hopes, and instinctive knowledge which has been unfolding during recent years. When we think of these things, it seems as though spiritual science has been growing and developing without consciousness on the part of human beings, but that they were already dreaming of it, instinctively divining its approach. There are some, however, who have pondered about the spiritual life, and they have indicated what they felt concerning the rhythmic recurrence of phenomena and even concerning the return of the human soul.

It is interesting, here, to speak of a case—which I could multiply a hundredfold—because it is an example of what is alive in all those who have contemplated the picture presented by human evolution and in their life of feeling have discerned the rhythmic recurrence, the rhythmic return of events. I will quote one example, which shows how this thought has taken root, causing something to spring to life in the soul. This writer could not have been a theosophist in the modern sense, for what I am going to refer to is a poem written in the year 1835. The writer could have had no knowledge of the vista of human evolution one day to be opened up by spiritual science. Yet something rises up in him that is like a dream of the future of humanity—an instinctive perception of recurrent phenomena in human existence. I am speaking of the poet Anastasius Grün,[†] who in the year 1835 published his work *Schutt* in which he depicts five recurrences of a certain happening, rhythmic repetitions of the spiritual message working in humanity. The poem depicts how on Easter Day, Christ re-visits the Mount of Olives in the spirit, in order to look again at the places where he had lived and suffered. The poem speaks of five returns, four of which lie in the past, and the fifth in the future. The first occurs in the period after the destruction of Jerusalem. The second, "when Christ beholds the conquest of Jerusalem by the Crusaders"; as he looks down, Christ sees what is happening in the places he had once known. The third return falls in the period when Islam was spreading its power over Jerusalem; the fourth in the period when humanity, split into countless sects, was quarrelling about the mission of Christ. All this is vividly and graphically described by Grün. Then there opens out the vista of a return of Christ on an Easter Day in the far-distant future. Although the picture is dreamlike and utopian, we cannot fail to discern—apart from the actual content of the poem—something of the blessing experienced by the soul when spiritual knowledge, especially as it has unfolded since the thirteenth century, opens up glimpses of a future when a spiritual culture will spread peace instead of wars and strife. Grün sees the blessings of peace in the culture of times to come and speaks of a future return of Christ to the Mount of Olives on an Easter Day, describing it as it appeared to his imagination. Children are playing on Golgotha; they have been digging in the ground and find a strange thing made of iron, not knowing at all what it can be; it proves, subsequently, to be a sword. And in the mood of exultation which comes upon him, Grün says that there will come a time when the very purpose of such an instrument as a sword will have been forgotten and the sword will be an object of amazement to men. Then he says that the iron will be used as a plough and describes the feeling which the rhythmic return of Christ to the Mount of Olives quickens in him. What has been forgotten and will again be revealed is a cross of stone! It is raised again and Grün says that something happens to the cross, indicating what part the cross will play hereafter. In the following verses he describes what feelings arise in him when the children unearth a cross and set it up for all the world to see—and he speaks, too, of the function and the power of the cross in mankind:

Ob sie's auch kennen nicht, doch steht's voll Segen,
Aufrecht in ihrer Brust, in ewigem Reiz.
Es blüht sein Name rings auf allen Wegen,
Denn, was sie nimmer kannten—war ein Kreuz!

Sie sahn den Kampf nicht und sein blutig Zeichen,
Sie sahn den Sieg allein und seinen Kranz!
Sie sahn den Sturm nicht mit den Wetterstreichen,
Sie sahn nur seines Regenbogens Glanz!

Das Kreuz von Stein, sie stellen's auf im Garten,
Ein rätselhaft ehrwürdig Altertum,
Dran Rosen rings und Blumen aller Arten
Empor sich ranken, kletternd um und um.

So steht das Kreuz inmitten Glanz und Fülle
Auf Golgotha, glorreich, bedeutungschwer:
Verdeckt ist's ganz von seiner Rosen Hülle,
Längst sieht vor Rosen man das Kreuz nicht mehr!

Though they know it not, it stands, all-blessing,
Upright within their breasts, ever beckoning,
Its seeds on every pathway grow and bloom;
For what they had never known—was a Cross!

They did not see the fight, its bloody sign,
They see alone the victory, its crown.
They did not see the storm, its thunderbolts,
They see alone its rainbow's wondrous glance!

The Cross of Stone, they place it in the garden,
A mystery of great antiquity,
Upon it, roses, flowers of every kind,
Entwine, climbing skyward round and round.

Thus stands the Cross mid splendor and profusion
On Golgotha, glorious, profound:
Wholly hidden by its rosy veil,
Men see no more the Cross, for roses there.[†]

Lecture Six

BERLIN, MAY 14, 1912

THE QUESTION AS to the meaning and purpose of existence frequently arises in life and in the sphere of philosophy. Study of spiritual science will certainly produce a kind of humility in regard to this question, for although we know that investigation of the spiritual worlds leads thought and perception beyond the material world of sense, we also realize that it is not possible to speak forthwith about the primal origins or the ultimate and highest meaning of life. The retort of superficial thinking here will certainly be: "What, then, *do* we know, if knowledge of the meaning and purpose of life is beyond our reach?"

An analogy that is entirely in line with the attitude of spiritual science and indicates what is permissible or not permissible in regard to this question can be put in the following way: Suppose a man wants to journey somewhere. In his home town he can only get information as to how to reach a much less distant place, but he is sent off with the assurance that once there, further help will be available. Although he makes inquiries here and there as he goes along, he cannot know the exact path which will bring him to his final destination; nevertheless, he is sure of arriving eventually because he is always able to find his way from place to place.

As students of spiritual science, we do not ask about the "ultimate goal" but about the one lying immediately ahead—in other words, about the goal of the Earth. We realize that it would be senseless to inquire about the "ultimate goal" for we have recognized that "evolution" is a reality in the life of man. It must therefore never be forgotten that at the present stage of our existence it is not possible to understand the goals of much later phases of evolution and that a higher vantage-point must be reached if we are to understand the meaning of a far-distant goal. And so we ask about the goal lying immediately ahead, realizing that by keeping it before us as an ideal and striving with the right means, we shall eventually attain it, thereby reaching a further stage in development. At that stage, it will be legitimate to ask about the "next" goal, and so on. Thus if it were ever suggested that spiritual science might tend to make a person arrogant because his outlook extends beyond the ordinary world into a spiritual world, in reality his attitude will be one of humility towards these sublime matters about which superficial questions are so often asked.

We inquire, to begin with, about the goal of the Earth. In other words: What is it that man adds, essentially, to the fruits of the preceding periods of Saturn, Sun, and Moon evolution, by developing on the Earth through repeated physical incarnations? We will here recall certain matters which will help us to associate concrete and definite ideas with what may be called the "meaning and purpose of Earth evolution." Let me speak, to begin with, of the following.

When intellectual thinking, based upon reason, came to birth during the Greco-Latin epoch—it would actually be true to say, in the sixth century BC—a certain thought found frequent utterance—namely, that all philosophy, all deeper contemplation upon the secrets of existence, proceeds from wonder, amazement. In other words, as long as the human being can feel no wonder at the phenomena of life around him, so long is his life vapid and thoughtless, and he asks without intelligence about the why and wherefore of existence. "All philosophy begins with wonder" was a much-quoted saying during the ancient Greco-Latin epoch. What, in reality, does it signify in man's life of soul?

It would be difficult today to find anyone in civilized Europe who has never set eyes on a locomotive in motion; not so very long ago, however, there were such persons—although nowadays they would, of course, only be found in very remote districts. If such a person sees a train moving along, he will feel wonder and amazement at the sight of an object going forward without any of the means with which he is acquainted. It is a known fact that many such people, in their astonishment at seeing a locomotive in movement, asked if the horses pulling it along were inside! Why were the people cast into amazement and wonder by what they saw here? It was because they were looking at something which in a certain sense was known, and at the same time unknown to them. They knew that things move forward, but whatever they had seen had always been provided with quite a different means of movement. Now they were looking at something on which they had never set eyes before. And this gave rise to wonder.

If during the Greco-Latin epoch, people could only become philosophers when they were capable of wonder, they must have been individuals who perceived, in everything taking place in the world, something at once known and unknown, in so far as the happenings and phenomena seemed to contain more than appeared on the surface—something unknown to them.

Why had the attitude of the philosophers to be that the primary causes and certain attributes of things in the world lay in a sphere unknown to them? As it will be admitted that philosophers are at least as clever as people who give no thought at all to what goes on around them, it cannot be supposed that philosophers are capable of accepting only what is to be perceived by means of the ordinary senses. Therefore, they must find something lacking—or rather, they must surmise the presence of something which sets them wondering—something that is not present in the world of sense. And so, before the days of materialism, the philosophers always sought for the *suprasensory* in the phenomena presented to the senses. The wonder felt by the philosophers, therefore, is associated with the fact that certain things are not to be comprehended through what presents itself to the eyes of sense. They said to themselves: "What I there perceive does not tally with what I picture it to be; I must therefore conceive that suprasensory forces are present within it." But in the world of sense the philosophers perceived no suprasensory forces. That alone is enough to make a thinking man realize that a subconscious memory, not reaching into consciousness, has persisted in the human being since times when the soul perceived something more than the actual phenomena of the sense world. In other words, remembrance arises of experiences undergone before the descent into sense existence. It is as though the soul were to say: "I discern things and their effects which can only call forth wonder in me, because they are different from what I have seen before; enlightenment about them can only be found by means of forces which must be drawn from the suprasensory world." And so all philosophizing begins with wonder, because in reality man approaches the phenomena of existence as a being who comes into the world of the senses from a suprasensory world and finds that the things of the sense world do not tally with what he perceived in the suprasensory world. Wonder arises in him when the form in which the things of sense are made manifest can only be explained by knowledge he once possessed in a suprasensory world. And so wonder points to the connection of man with the suprasensory world, to something belonging to a sphere he can only enter when he transcends the world in which his physical body encloses him. This is one indication of the fact that here, in this physical world, there is a continual urge within the human being to reach out beyond himself. Someone who can only remain shut up in himself, who is not driven by wonder beyond the field of the I, of the ordinary I, remains one who cannot reach beyond himself, who sees the sun rise and set without a thought and with complete unconcern. This is the kind of existence led by uncivilized peoples.

A second power which releases the human being from the ordinary world, leading him at once away from material perception into suprasensory insight, is compassion, fellow-feeling (of this, too, I have spoken). Those who go heedlessly through the world do not regard compassion as having any great mystery about it; but to the thoughtful, compassion is a great and mysterious secret. When we look at a being only from outside, impressions come from him to our senses and intellect; with the awakening of compassion, we pass beyond the sphere of these impressions. We share in what is taking place in his innermost nature, and transcending the sphere of our own I, we pass over into *his* world. In other words, we are set free from ourselves, we break through the barriers of ordinary existence in the physical body and reach over into the other being. Here, already, is the suprasensory—for neither the operations of the senses nor of the reasoning mind can carry us into the sphere of another's soul. The fact that compassion exists in the world bears witness that even in the world of sense we can be set free from, can pass out beyond ourselves and enter into the world of another being. If a person is incapable of compassion, there is a moral defect, a moral lack in him. If at the moment when he should get free from himself and pass over into the other being—feeling not his own pain or joy but the pain or joy of that other—if at that moment his feelings fade and die away, then something is lacking in his moral life. The human being on Earth, if he is to reach the stature of full and complete humanity, must be able to pass out beyond his own earthly life, he must be able to live in another, not only in himself.

Conscience is a third power whereby the human being transcends what he is in the physical body. In ordinary life he will desire this or that; according to his impulses or needs, he will pursue what is pleasing and thrust aside what is displeasing to him. But in many such actions he will be his own critic, in that his conscience, the voice of his conscience, sounds a note of correction. Final satisfaction or dissatisfaction with what he has done also depends upon how the voice of conscience has spoken. This in itself is a proof that "conscience" is a power whereby the human being is led out beyond the sphere of his impulses, his likes and dislikes.

Wonder and amazement, compassion or fellow-feeling, conscience—these are the three powers by means of which the human being, even while in the physical body, transcends his own limitations, for through these powers, influences which cannot find entrance into the human soul by way of the intellect and the senses, ray into physical life.

It is easy to understand that these three powers can only unfold through incarnations in a body of flesh. Man must, as it were, be kept separate by a body of flesh from what pours into his life of soul from another sphere. If a body of flesh did not separate him from the spiritual world and present the outer world to him as a sense world, he would be incapable of wonder. It is the material body which enables wonder at the things of the world of sense to arise in man, compelling him to seek for the spirit. Compassion could not unfold if the one human being were not separated from the other, if human beings were to live an undivided existence in which a single flow of spiritual life pervaded the consciousness of them all, if each soul were not separated from other souls by the impenetrable sheath provided by the physical body. And conscience could not be experienced as a spiritual force, sending its voice into man's world of natural urges, passions, and desires, if the material body did not hanker after things against which warning must be given by another power. And so the human being must be incarnated in a physical body in order that he may be able to experience wonder, compassion, and conscience.

In our time, people concern themselves little with such secrets, although they are profoundly enlightening. But in a past by no means very remote, a great deal of attention was paid to these things.

Think only of the world of the Greek gods, the gods of Homer; think of their actions and activities; try to understand the nature of the impulses working in Achilles, a being who stands there like a last survivor of an earlier generation on Earth. He, too, was born of a divine mother. Read through the *Iliad* and the *Odyssey* and ask yourselves whether this being, standing halfway between gods and men, was ever stirred by anything like "conscience" or "compassion"? Homer builds the whole of the *Iliad* around the fury of the "wrath" of Achilles—and wrath is a passion. Everything in the Greek legend centers around this; the *Iliad* tells of what came about as the result of a passion—the wrath of Achilles. Consider all the deeds of Achilles described in the *Iliad* and see if you can say of a single one that Achilles is here moved by anything like compassion or conscience. Neither is there a single example of the stirring of wonder. The very greatness of Homer lies in his power to depict these things with such sublimity. When Achilles is told of some terrible happening, his behavior is far from that of a man filled with wonder. And then turn to the Greek gods themselves: they give vent to all kinds of impulses which are certainly of the nature of egotism when they manifest in a human being enclosed in a physical body. In the gods they are spiritual impulses. But among the Greek Gods there is no compassion, no suggestion of conscience, nor anything like wonder. Why not? Because Homer and the Greeks knew that these gods were beings belonging to a period of evolution preceding that of the Earth—a period when the beings who were then passing through their "human stage" under the conditions prevailing in existence, had not yet received into the life of soul the powers of wonder, compassion, and conscience. It must be constantly remembered that the earlier planetary conditions through which the Earth has passed and in which such beings as the Greek gods underwent their human stage, were not there for the purpose of implanting wonder, compassion, and conscience in the life of soul. That is precisely the mission of Earth evolution! The purpose of Earth evolution is that there may be implanted into the evolutionary process as a whole, powers which could otherwise never have come into existence: wonder, compassion, and conscience.

I have told you how the birth of conscience can clearly be traced to a certain period of Greek culture. In the works of Aeschylus, what we call "conscience" played no part; there were only remembrances of the avenging Furies, and not until we come to the works of Euripedes is there any clear expression of conscience as we know it now. The concept of conscience arose only very gradually during the Greco-Latin epoch. I have told you that the concept of wonder arises for the first time when men begin to philosophize in the world of Greco-Latin culture. And a remarkable fact in the spiritual evolution of Earth existence throws far-reaching light upon what we know as compassion and also, in the true sense, love. In the age of materialism, it is exceedingly difficult to maintain, in true and right perspective, this concept of compassion or love. Many of you will realize that in our materialistic times, this concept is distorted, in that materialism associates the concept of "love" so closely with that of "sexuality"—with which, fundamentally, it has nothing whatever to do. That is a point where the culture of our day abandons both intelligence and sound, healthy reason. Through its materialism, evolution in our time is veering not only towards the unintelligent and illogical but even towards the scandalous, when "love" is dragged into such close association with what is covered by the term "sexuality." The fact that under certain circumstances the element of sexuality may be associated with love between man and woman is no argument for bringing so closely together the all-embracing nature of love or compassion and the entirely specific character of sexuality. So far as logic is concerned, to associate the concept of, say, a "locomotive" with that of a man being "run over," because locomotives do sometimes run people over, would be just about as intelligent as it is to connect the concept of love so closely with that of sexuality—simply because under certain circumstances there is an outward association. That this happens today is not the outcome of any scientific hypothesis but of the irrational and, to some extent, unhealthy mode of thinking prevailing in our time.

On the other hand, another telling fact points to the significance inherent in the concept of love and compassion. At a certain point in the evolution of humanity, and among all peoples, something is made manifest which, while differing in many essentials, is identical in one respect all over the Earth—namely, in the adoption of the concept of love, of compassion. It is very remarkable that six or seven centuries before the inpouring of the Christ-impulse into humanity, founders of religion and systems of thought appeared all over the Earth, among all the peoples. It is of the highest significance that, six centuries before our era, Laozi and Confucius should have been living in China, the Buddha in India, the last Zarathustra (*not* the original Zarathustra) in Persia, and Pythagoras in Greece. How great the difference is between these founders of religion! Only a mind abstracted from reality and incapable of discerning the differences can suggest, as is often mischievously done today, that the teachings of Laozi or Confucius do not differ from those of other founders of religions. Yet in one respect there is similarity among them all; they all teach that compassion and love must reign between soul and soul! The point of significance is this: six centuries before our era, consciousness begins to stir that love and compassion are to be received into the stream of human evolution. Thus, whether we are thinking of the birth of wonder, of conscience, or of love and compassion in the stream of evolution, all the signs point to the fact that in the fourth post-Atlantean epoch of culture, something was imbued into mankind which we may recognize as the "meaning and purpose of Earth evolution."

How superficial and foolish it is when people say: "Why was it necessary for man to come down from the worlds of divine spirit into the physical world, only to have to reattain them? Why could he not have remained in the higher worlds?" Man could not remain in those worlds because only by coming down into the physical world of Earth evolution could he receive into himself the forces of wonder, love or compassion, and conscience or moral responsibility.

We look at the fourth post-Atlantean epoch of culture and perceive, during its course, the dawn of impulses which—in reality only from that time onwards—spread more and more widely among mankind. It is very easy today to emphasize how seldom humanity is ruled by compassion and love, how seldom by conscience. But in pointing to these things, we must also be mindful of the fact that in the Greco-Latin age, slavery was still an accepted custom, and that even a philosopher as great as Aristotle still regarded the existence of slaves as a necessary principle of human life; we must also remember that since those days, love has so far gained ground that even if today inequalities still persist among human beings, there is already present in their souls something like a feeling of shame that certain conditions exist. This in itself indicates that the forces which entered at that time into evolution are unfolding within human souls. Nobody would dare nowadays—if he is to avoid the tragic fate of Nietzsche[†] (the "followers" of Nietzsche can be ignored altogether, for in his right mind Nietzsche would have repudiated them)—to stand openly for the introduction of slavery as it was in Greece. Nobody will deny that the greatest of all forces in the human soul is that of love and compassion, and that it must be man's task to ever refine the voice that sounds out of another world into the soul.

Holding firmly in our minds that the unfolding of the three powers described constitutes the meaning and purpose of Earth evolution, we turn to the greatest of all impulses—the Christ-impulse which poured into evolution during the fourth post-Atlantean epoch. Even outer circumstances indicate that this impulse is given at the very time when the Earth is ready for the development of the three powers of wonder, compassion or love, and conscience, or moral responsibility, as intrinsically *human* qualities. Many studies have given us a picture of how the Christ-impulse made its way into the evolution of humanity.

I want here to refer to one aspect of the Christ-impulse. I have told you that certain spiritual, superhuman forces were held back in the spiritual worlds at the beginning of the evolutionary process on the

Earth. This impulse streamed into the Earth at the time of which an indication is given in the Bible—namely, at the time of the Baptism in the Jordan. It was an impulse, therefore, untouched by the luciferic forces as it had been kept back until the fourth post-Atlantean epoch; in that epoch it streamed into humanity. And now think of this in connection with certain things we have ourselves experienced. If people are incapable of giving any concrete explanation of how the spiritual world plays into the physical world, it is really out of place for them to come out with crude and unreal ideas, such as, for example, that of the "Three Logoi." I have said many times that the word "Logoi" can convey to the ordinary intelligence nothing more than its five letters. When it is alleged in certain quarters outside that here we speak of Christ as the "second Logos," we do well to realize that misrepresentation and distortion are the order of the day. We ourselves are quoted as the source of statements which have actually originated somewhere else! Our constant endeavor is to deepen, to widen and to gather from every side, knowledge that can shed light on the Christ-idea. Yet outside our field of work, by talking round an abstract concept, people allege that we speak of the Christ as the "Second Logos." In the Theosophical Society, conscience ought to be too sharp to permit such allegations. So long as sheer misrepresentation of other people's views is possible, the theosophical movement cannot be said to have reached any particularly high level, and while this sort of thing goes on, it is futile to boast about freedom of opinion in the Society. This is an empty phrase as long as people allow themselves to spread false ideas of the views held by others. Certainly, there must be freedom to spread every shade of opinion—but not freedom to misrepresent the views of others! Spiritual conscience must be sharpened in this respect; otherwise, all feeling for truth would in the end be driven out of the theosophical movement and then it would not be possible to cultivate the true spiritual movement within the framework of the "theosophical movement." These things must not be glossed over but taken really seriously. Certainly, there may be fewer publications, if the aim is to print only those things which are founded upon genuine, reliable knowledge. But after all, what harm will be done if there is less printing? What does it matter if less is said, so long as *what* is said is true and in accordance with reality? It was recently stated in periodicals abroad that the Christ is spoken of by us as the "Second Logos" and that we are said to be cultivating a "narrow" theosophy, suitable for Germany, but not for any other country; we are said to be cultivating a "narrow" theosophy, whereas a really "broad" theosophical movement is being conducted from a certain center in Leipzig of which you have heard. When things of this kind are to be read, it can only be concluded that there does not exist in the theosophical movement the sharpness of conscience that is the prerequisite of a spiritual movement. And if we lack this sharpness of conscience, if we do not feel the most intense responsibility to the holiest truth, we shall make no progress on any other path. These things have to be said. And within the theosophical movement, it will above all be necessary to have eyes for the quality of love and compassion.

If we conceive the Christ-impulse to be the downpouring of that spiritual power which was kept back in the ancient Lemurian time in order to flow into evolution during the fourth post-Atlantean epoch at the point marked by the Baptism in the Jordan, reaching its culmination in the Mystery of Golgotha—then it is clear that he who is known as the "Christ" was not, even at that time, incarnated in the ordinary sense, in a physical human being. We know what complicated processes were connected with the man "Jesus of Nazareth" in order that for three years of his life the Christ-impulse might live within him. We are therefore able to understand that for three years the Christ-impulse lived on the Earth in the three sheaths of a human being, but we realize, too, that even at that time, the Christ-impulse was not "incarnated" on the Earth in the ordinary sense but that he "pervaded" the body of the being "Jesus of Nazareth." This must be understood when it is said that it is not possible to speak of a "return" of Christ, but only of an impulse which was present once, during the time of the events in Palestine beginning with the Baptism in the Jordan, when there remained only the physical body, the etheric body, and the astral body of Jesus of Nazareth; within these sheaths the Christ was then present on the very soil of the Earth. From that time Christ has been united with the spiritual atmosphere of the Earth and can there be found by souls who are willing to receive him. From that time onwards—and only from that time onwards—he has been present in the spiritual atmosphere of the Earth. The great turn given to Earth evolution lies in the fact that from that time forward there was a power in the Earth which it did not previously contain.

We know that what we actually see in the kingdoms of nature around us is not reality, but *maya*, the great illusion. In the kingdom of the animals, we see the individual forms coming into being and passing away; the group soul alone endures. In the plant kingdom, the individual plants appear and disappear, but behind them there is the Earth-spirit which does not pass away. So it is, too, in the kingdom of the minerals. The spiritual endures, but the physical, whether in the animal, plant or mineral kingdom, is transient, impermanent. Even the outer senses discern that the planet Earth is involved in a process of pulverization and will at some future time disintegrate into dust. We have spoken of how the body of the Earth will be cast off by the spirit of the Earth, as the human body is cast off by the individual human spirit. What will remain as the highest substance of the Earth when its goal has been reached? The Christ-impulse was present on the Earth as "spiritual substance," so to speak. He endures and will be received into human beings during the course of Earth evolution. But how does he live on? When he was upon the Earth for three years, he had no physical body, no etheric body, no astral body of his own, but was enveloped in the three sheaths of Jesus of Nazareth. When the Earth has reached its goal, it will, like man, be a fully developed being fit for the Christ-impulse.

But from whence are the three sheaths of the Christ-impulse derived? From forces that can be unfolded only on the Earth. Beginning with the Mystery of Golgotha, whatever has unfolded on the Earth since the fourth post-Atlantean period as the power of wonder—whatever comes to life in us as wonder—passes, finally, to the Christ, weaving the astral body of the Christ-impulse. Love or compassion in human souls weaves the etheric body of the Christ-impulse; and the power of conscience, which from the time of the Mystery of Golgotha until the goal of the Earth is attained lives in and inspires human souls, weaves the physical body—or what corresponds with the physical body—for the Christ-impulse.

The true meaning of the words from the Gospel can only now be discerned: "Inasmuch as ye have done it unto one of the least of these my brethren, ye have done it unto me" (Matt. 25:40). Here we have characterized how Christ feels what flows from man to man as the successive individual atoms of his own etheric body: what is developed as love or compassion weaves into the etheric body of Christ. Thus, when the goal of Earth evolution is attained, he will be enveloped by that which has lived in human beings and which, when they have moved beyond their I, will become the sheaths of Christ.

And now think of how human beings live in communion with Christ. From the time of the Mystery of Golgotha to the attainment of the goal of Earth evolution, man grows more perfect in that he develops to the stature that is within his reach as a being endowed with the power of the I. But men are united with the Christ who has come among them, in that they transcend their own I and—through wonder—build the astral body of Christ. Christ does not build his own astral body, but in the wonder that arises in their souls, human beings share in the forming of the astral body of Christ. His etheric body will be fashioned through the compassion and love flowing from man to man, and his "physical body" through the power of conscience unfolding in human beings. Whatever wrongs are committed in these three realms deprive the Christ of the possibility of full development on the Earth—that is to say, Earth evolution is left imperfect. Those who go about the Earth with indifference and unconcern, who have no urge to understand what the Earth can reveal to them, deprive the astral body of Christ of the possibility of full development; those who live without unfolding compassion and love, hinder the etheric body of Christ from full development; and those who lack conscience hinder the development of what corresponds with the physical body of Christ—but this means that the Earth cannot reach the goal of its evolution.

The principle of egotism has to be overcome in Earth evolution. The Christ-impulse penetrates more and more deeply into the life and culture of humanity, and the conviction that this impulse has lived its way into mankind, free from every trace of denominationalism—as, for example, in the paintings of Raphael—this conviction will bear its fruit. How Christ may truly be portrayed is a problem still to be solved. People on Earth will have to be greatly enriched in their life of feeling if, after the many attempts made through the centuries, another is to succeed to some slight extent in expressing what the Christ is as the suprasensory impulse living on through Earth evolution. The attempts made hitherto do not even suggest what form such a portrayal of Christ should take. For it would have to express how the enveloping sheaths woven of the forces of wonder, compassion, and conscience are gradually made manifest. The countenance of Christ must be so vital and living that it is an expression of the victory won over the sensory, desire-nature in earthly human beings—victory achieved through the very forces which have spiritualized the countenance. There must be sublime power in this countenance. The painter or sculptor will have to express in the unusual form of the chin and mouth, the power of conscience unfolded to its highest degree. The mouth must convey the impression that it is not there for the purpose of taking food but to give utterance to whatever moral strength and power of conscience has been cultivated by humanity through the ages; the very structure of the bones around the teeth in the lower jaw will seem to form themselves into a mouth. All this will have to be expressed in the countenance. The form of the lower part of the face will have to express a power whose outstreaming rays seem to shatter the rest of the human body into pieces, changing this body into another form through which certain other forces are overcome, so that it will be impossible to give Christ, who will have a mouth like this, a bodily form similar to that possessed by the physical human being today. On the other hand, all the power of compassion will flow out of his eyes—the power that eyes alone can contain—not in order to receive impressions but to bear the very soul into the joys and sufferings of others. His brow will give no suggestion of thought based upon earthly sense impressions. It will be a brow conspicuously prominent above the eyes, arching over that part of the brain; it will not be a "thinker's" brow which merely works upon material already there. Wonder will be made manifest in this projecting brow which curves gently backwards over the head, expressing wonder and marvel at the mysteries of the world. It will be a head such as is nowhere to be found in physical humanity.

Every true representation of the Christ must be a portrayal of the Ideal embodied in Him. When man reaches out towards this highest Ideal and strives through spiritual science to represent it in art, this feeling will arise in greater and greater strength: If you would portray the Christ, you must not look at what is actually there in the world, but you must let your whole being be quickened and pervaded by all that flows from contemplation of the spiritual evolution of the world, inspired by the three great impulses of wonder, compassion, and conscience.

Lecture Seven

BERLIN, MAY 20, 1912

THE LAST LECTURE dealt with the subject of how the Christ-impulse will unfold in future times, and also, of course, in our own epoch. We heard that sheaths will weave themselves as it were around the Christ-impulse: wonder into an astral body; feelings of love or compassion into an etheric body; the power of conscience into what corresponds to a physical body. Thereby that ideal being whose I—the Christ-impulse itself—passed into the Earth through the Mystery of Golgotha will reach completion in the course of the time still remaining to Earth evolution. The fundamental character of the future ideal of humanity was described in one of its aspects and the present lecture will endeavor to add yet another, different picture.

The Christ-impulse came, so to speak, in the middle of the age following upon the great Atlantean catastrophe. This age may be said to extend from the time of the Atlantean catastrophe to the next great catastrophe of which you may read in the lectures on the Apocalypse.† In the middle of this period, the most important of all events in Earth evolution takes place—the coming of the Christ-impulse. As the last lecture indicated, it is not necessary to turn our eyes to Palestine in order to realize that something of the highest importance was taking place at that time in Earth evolution. We have only to study the Greco-Latin epoch of culture, lying as it does in the middle of the post-Atlantean period, and recall one of its characteristic features; this, again, can be compared with a similar feature in the preceding Third epoch and in our own epoch.

The essential and fundamental character of a Greek temple has often been described. Its form stands there as a complete, self-contained, independent whole, even when it is not actually before our eyes, even when we conceive of no human being anywhere near it. Inside a Greek temple, human beings always seem to be a disturbing element; they do not really belong to it, they do not belong inside it. For what, in reality, is a Greek temple? We can only understand it in its whole form and structure if we think of it as the dwelling-place of a living, invisible god who has come down to the physical plane. That is the reason why every temple is dedicated to one particular god. And when we picture the god in the temple—with no human beings present—the god for whom a dwelling place has been built on Earth, then we have grasped the "idea" embodied in the Greek temple. Human beings really have no place there. This was the idea underlying the whole architecture of a Greek temple. Such architecture could only arise in an epoch when the divine-spiritual was known to pervade all existence on the physical plane. People whose paths appeared to be everywhere steeped in the divine could feel all the depth of meaning contained in words uttered by one of them: "Better it is to be a beggar in the Upper World than a king in the realm of the Shades!" That is to say, in the world lying on the other side of the gate of death. It was the period when human beings experienced, in greatest intensity, their union with the physical plane and with the spiritual pervading the physical plane.

Let us compare a Greek temple with a building of the same character in the preceding epoch—and with buildings which, in our own epoch, indicate its fundamental attitude and trend. Think of an Egyptian temple, even of the pyramids: they become intelligible only when we see them as expressions of man's aspiration to the divine—to the divine Godhead who has not yet descended to the physical plane. In the architecture of the Egyptian time, every line, every form, expresses the striving of man towards the divine-spiritual. But these mysterious and deeply symbolical buildings indicate in themselves that men must have undergone preparation before the architectural forms could help them to find the way to the divine-spiritual. They needed preparation: they needed to have reached the first stage of initiation. The same applies to the architecture of Asia Minor. In our own epoch, Gothic architecture gives the keynote. This is an occult fact. It is impossible to have the same conception of a Gothic cathedral as of a Greek temple; for a Gothic cathedral is incomplete without the congregation of believers. It is simply not complete without the human beings within it! All its forms seem to convey that they are there to receive the prayers of the believers—the *believers*, in contrast to the *initiates* in ancient Egypt. Anyone who can discern what these things mean realizes from the course taken by the evolution of form from the Egyptian temple, through the Greek temple, to the Gothic cathedral, that the impulse leading to the unfolding of the human I entered at a certain point into the process of earthly existence. Wherever we look, we can perceive how the Christ-impulse lays hold of man, leaves its stamp and signature upon all happenings, all development, and it seems grotesque when philosophical or theological thought declares that acceptance of such an impulse rests upon the basis of historical records. It does not rest upon any historical record whatever, but simply and solely upon a discerning, clear-sighted observation of human evolution; for no matter where we look, we see that evolution follows the same course as that revealed in architecture. The initiate who alone was capable of understanding the architectural forms of the Egypto-Chaldean epoch—the third post-Atlantean epoch—knew that he must raise himself above the level of ordinary human nature: then and only then could he ascend into the region of divine-spiritual life. The initiate of the fourth post-Atlantean epoch knew that in the *physical* world he was living together with the divine, but he had very little connection with what the Greeks called the World of Shades, because by that time man had descended more deeply into physical existence. And when the gods did not mingle with men in the temples, the Greeks felt no connection with that other world.

Since the fourth post-Atlantean epoch, these conditions have changed—changed in the sense that it is possible now for every single soul to find the path to the divine-spiritual. It is extremely important to realize this, for it is the most concrete expression of the fact that in ancient times men were much nearer to the spiritual in their consciousness, in their knowledge, and in their life of soul. Then came the descent to the physical plane and now there must be a gradual re-ascent. We are living in the age when the re-ascent must be undertaken *consciously*—whereas, to begin with, the Christ-impulse worked unconsciously in men.

Our own epoch is a kind of recapitulation of the Egypto-Chaldean period. Of the Greco-Latin epoch there is no recapitulation, for it lies in the middle of the seven consecutive periods. The third epoch is being recapitulated, in a certain form, in our own age; the second epoch, that of ancient Persian culture, will be recapitulated in the sixth epoch, which will follow our own; and in the far-distant seventh epoch, before a stupendous catastrophe, the first epoch, that of ancient Indian culture, will be recapitulated—not, of course, in the same form, for the recapitulation will everywhere bear the imprint of the Christ-impulse.

A certain consciousness existed, especially in olden times, of what has come to pass in the evolution of mankind. Ancient times, of course, were especially conscious of the descent of humanity, the descent to the physical plane from the heights of divine-spiritual existence. But for every process, there must be a preparation. There had been a preparation, too, for the impulse given by the Mystery of Golgotha in the fourth epoch—the impulse for the re-ascent. This impulse had its "forerunners"—in Elijah, John the Baptist, and others. But consciousness of the fact that mankind has descended from divine-spiritual existence and in the future must re-ascend into the worlds of divine spirit was present not only in the culture which eventually made its way into the West; evidence of such consciousness is to be found in every civilization.

A very widespread and characteristic idea finds expression in the traditions of practically all peoples—an idea which can, it is true, be applied widely, but which in its final phase is to be associated with a definite and specific tradition. It is a tradition upon which there has been much reflection and upon which occult knowledge alone can shed light—namely, the tradition of the Flood. Much that is connected with this tradition refers, of course, to far earlier times, but the following is brought clearly to light by occult investigation. Nearly all the peoples who have left reliable historical records or legends refer to the Flood as having taken place about three thousand years before the Mystery of Golgotha; that is the period indicated by the legends. There is not enough time today to explain why this last Flood, which was supposed to have occurred three thousand years before our era, cannot be taken to indicate a great physical catastrophe or deluge. Obviously, it does not refer to the Atlantean catastrophe, for that took place very much earlier. The "Flood," therefore, must mean something entirely different. Yet the fact should not be lost sight of that the traditions of all the peoples in question place the Flood in the fourth millennium before our era. Although the dates vary a little, they tally in the main essentials.

At this point, I will ask you to remember that in the first post-Atlantean epoch, when the Holy Rishis were the great teachers of humanity, culture was inspired primarily by the human etheric body; during the ancient Persian epoch, culture was inspired by the astral body, the sentient body; in the Egypto-Chaldean epoch by the sentient soul; in the Greco-Latin epoch by the mind or intellectual soul; in our present epoch by the consciousness soul. And now the time is approaching when the powers of the spirit self will gradually be imbued into culture. In that evolution proceeded in this way, the experiences arising in man's life of soul underwent deep and far-reaching change. Just think of it. The picture of the world presented to a man of the earliest Indian epoch, of which even the Vedas have no knowledge, received its essential character and stamp from the working of the etheric body. Through the etheric body man cannot direct his gaze to the outer world in the way that is customary in our time. His perception, his picture of the world cannot be as it is today; where the forces of the etheric body are in operation, everything arises from *within*. A person of today can only have an idea—dim and lifeless at that—of perception that derives from the etheric body when he recalls the character of his dreams. But the dreams and visions through which, during the ancient Indian epoch, one human being became known to another, were living and real in the very highest degree. To imagine that when one human being met another, the outer perception of him was the same as it is today, would be quite erroneous. The man of ancient India saw pictures—but in those times the other human being physically before him was enveloped in an auric cloud, shrouded in a kind of mist. The character of perception was altogether different compared with perception as it is at the present day; these pictures, although full of the greatest spiritual import, were blurred and hazy. The forces streaming down from cosmic space, from the world of the stars—it was these forces that were seen in such clarity and brilliance in those ancient times. In the second post-Atlantean epoch, the power to look outwards gradually unfolded but, strangely enough, the faculty for gazing into the great cosmic spaces remained. Whereas perceptions of the world below were still hazy and without definition, the ancient Persian gazed with lucid clarity into the world of the stars. It is therefore intelligible that Zarathustrianism should point directly to cosmic space, to the light of the Sun, to Ahura Mazdao, or Ormuzd. This was because the astral body was primarily active. By the end of the ancient Persian epoch, the faculty of looking outwards into the physical world was already in its preparatory stage. The impulses leading to perception as it is in our day have been developing for long, long ages. Thus, the impulse to look out into the physical world was gradually instilled into man, leading him to the entirely new mode of perception which began to light up by slow degrees.

When the ancient Persian epoch was drawing to its close and the next period was glimmering like a dawn of the future, people felt: "We shall no longer be able to experience with such intensity the divine heritage that has come to us from the olden days of Atlantis, when with their power of inner, clairvoyant vision, men lived in communion with the worlds of divine spirit." The gaze was turned *back to the past.* What mattered most for these people were their remembrances in which living pictures arose like dreams—dreams of how the gods had fashioned the world through the ages of Lemuria and Atlantis. They felt that these remembrances were withdrawing, were fading away from humanity and that conditions were approaching when man must work with a faculty which tells him of the outer world, clouds the bright light of the inner world of the spirit, and compels him to look from within outwards, if he is to master the external world. This age was drawing nearer and nearer. Those who had the deepest, clearest perception of the dawn of the new epoch were people who at that time were the initiates in ancient India. They felt it in the form, as it were, of a divine impulse, compelling the human being to think for himself, through inner activity, about what confronts him in the physical world to which he was descending. Picturing this impulse as a divine being, the successors of the first, very ancient Indian culture—those who were living now during the second post-Atlantean epoch—called this being "Pramati." These people felt: "The god Pramati is drawing near, snatching human beings away from the guidance given by the ancient gods; Pramati is causing the disappearance of everything which ancient clairvoyance revealed concerning the world and is forcing man to look outwards into the physical plane. Darkness is creeping over the world of the ancient gods. A time is approaching when in their life of soul men will no longer be able to gaze into the world of the gods but will only turn their eyes to the outer world. Kali Yuga, the 'Black Age' is approaching; the bright age of ancient divinity is giving place to the age when the gods of old withdraw. It is the age inaugurated by the god Pramati!"

Kali Yuga was said to begin at a time which lies 3,101 years before our own era; this is the time of the Flood according to Indian tradition. For it was said that the Flood coincides with the coming of Kali Yuga, and Kali Yuga was conceived to be the offspring of the god Pramati.

Kali Yuga broke in upon the world, reaching its close in our own age. Now that the ascent to the spiritual world must begin, a spiritual science has come to mankind. Kali Yuga began 3,101 years before our era and ended in the year 1899 AD. That is why 1899 is a year of such importance. The re-ascent to the spiritual worlds—this must be the ideal of the future.

The age preceding the onset of Kali Yuga was, however, an age characteristic of the ancient Persian epoch when the old remembrances rose up within man via the astral body. Now he was to turn to the world outside. This was a great and epoch-making transition. In the case of many human beings, it came about in such a way that for a time all vision departed from them and darkness spread over their souls. This condition of darkness did not last for long periods, actually only for weeks. But people passed into this condition of sleep, and many never came out of it. Many of them perished and only relatively few were left in widely scattered regions. There is not enough time today to describe the conditions actually prevailing at that time. It can only be said briefly that owing to so large a number of human beings having succumbed, conditions were dark and sinister in the extreme and at only a few scattered places did people awaken from the great spiritual deluge that spread over their souls like a sleep. This condition of sleep was felt by most souls as a kind of "drowning" and by only a few as a re-awakening. And then came the "Black Age," the age devoid of the gods.

Were these things known to other human beings on the Earth? They were indeed. To our astonishment, we find widespread evidence of knowledge among the peoples that a deluge had submerged the consciousness of men and that in the third post-Atlantean epoch, through the development of the sentient soul—in other words, outward-turned vision—an entirely new power must have been inaugurated. The Indians divined this when they said: Kali Yuga is the offspring of Pramati. And what did the Greeks say? In Greece, "Pramati" becomes "Prometheus"—which is exactly the same. Prometheus is the brother of Epimetheus. The latter represents one who still "looks back" into ancient times. Epimetheus is the one whose thoughts turn backward; Prometheus sends his thoughts forward, to the world outside, to what takes place there. Just as Pramati has his offspring in Kali Yuga, so, too, Prometheus has his offspring. The Greek form of "Kali Yuga" is "Kalion." And because the Greeks felt it to be the age of Darkness, the "d" is prefixed and the word becomes "Deukalion"—which is really the same word as "Kali Yuga." This is not ingenious fancy, but an occult fact. It is clear, therefore, that the Greeks possessed the same knowledge as the Indian sages. This is quoted merely as an example, indicating that in their conditions of old clairvoyance, knowledge of these truths came to human beings and they were able to express them in majestic pictures. The Greek legend tells how, on the advice of his father Prometheus, Deukalion builds a wooden chest; in this he and his wife Pyrrha alone are saved from destruction when Zeus proposes to exterminate the human race by a deluge. Deukalion and Pyrrha land on Parnassus, and from them issues the new human race. Deukalion is the son of Prometheus—and in the intervening period comes the flood, denoting among manifold peoples, a *condition of consciousness.*

These wonderful pictures, which have been preserved in the traditions of so many of the peoples, show us how truths concerning the evolution of mankind have survived among them.

As humanity lived on gradually into the age of Kali Yuga, into the third post-Atlantean epoch, the ancient clairvoyant knowledge faded away. We who have to recapitulate the third epoch, must bring this kind of knowledge to life once again, but in an entirely new form. The lecture given a fortnight ago dealt with this subject. Western culture, the beginnings of which were mingled with the ancient Hebrew culture, has to concentrate primary attention on the single personality living on the physical plane between birth and death; Western culture cannot focus its main attention on the individuality who passes through the different epochs, but concentrates upon the existence of the one personality, whose life between birth and death runs its course on the physical plane, not in the higher worlds. Now that Kali Yuga has come to an end, consciousness must be imbued with the forces necessary for the further evolution of the human race; what was lost during Kali Yuga must be raised again from the depths. Our eyes must be directed more and more to the on-flowing life of the individuality. I have spoken of a series of lives in the West—Elijah, John the Baptist, Raphael, Novalis—and have shown how, by the addition of knowledge derived from the spiritual worlds, we can perceive the continuous thread of the soul, the on-flowing life of the one individuality in Elijah, John the Baptist, Raphael, Novalis.

In our spiritual movement, development of this insight must be a *conscious* aspiration, for it is a necessity in the evolution and culture of the Earth. No progress would be possible by the mere continuation of the old experiences, the old knowledge. I have emphasized often enough all that it means for the human mind to enrich and make fruitful the heritage of ancient times by means of the new knowledge now available. It must, however, be realized that just as the transition from life inspired by the astral body to a spiritual life of soul, primarily in the sentient soul, was fraught with deep significance, so, now, we must work our way from life in the consciousness soul to life in the spirit self. I have intimated how this will take place by saying that during the next three thousand years, an increasing number of human beings will experience the appearance of the Christ-impulse, will be able to experience the Christ-impulse in the spiritual worlds. But actual realization of the influences streaming in from the spiritual world will have to unfold in greater intensity in the times lying ahead of us. It will not suffice to know in a general way, in theory, that the human being lives on after death; man's whole picture of life must carry the sure conviction that when the human being passes through the gate of death, he lives on still, death being merely a transition. We must realize, not as a theory but as actual knowledge, that while a human being is alive, he works upon us physically, through his body; after his death, he works spiritually, out of the spiritual world, upon our physical world. He is present in very truth. We must learn to see life in the light of such a fact and to reckon with what it involves.

Suppose it is our task to educate children. Anyone acquainted with these things is well aware that to educate children who up to their twentieth year still have parents living is a very different matter from having to educate children whose fathers died when they were four or five years old. When education is taken in deep earnestness, and the individuality of the child really studied (it is not a matter of speculation!)—especially in the case of a child whose father is dead, we shall often discern that there is something unusual at work here, something we cannot, at first, quite get hold of. Moreover, we shall not succeed in getting to the root of it by adopting the modes of thought drawn from materialism. But here and there the thought may occur: "Here is a strange current of the times. Most people regard those who belong to it as fools; but it may be worthwhile to find out what these theosophists have to say about the destiny of human beings after death. The theosophists tell us that although human beings discard their physical bodies at death, the content of their life of soul, their hopes, aspirations, and so forth, live on and are not inactive. Indeed, they are often more active after death than when the human being was living on the physical plane, enclosed in his body." Those who speak like this have paid attention to the results of spiritual research and will realize that the father is working upon the child from the spiritual world and, moreover, that he has definite hopes and longings which make their way into the life of the child! With this knowledge, success may come where it was not possible before, and we know how to deal with sympathies and antipathies which may express themselves in the child. To succeed with children, we need to know more than that the air affects them, and that when the air is chilly, they may catch cold. We must have knowledge of the influences playing from the spiritual world into the physical and of the form they take.

These things are still regarded as nonsense, but the time is not far distant when the very facts of life will compel people to take account of them and to reckon with what endures in the form of living and potent impulses after human beings have passed through death. Not until then will the concrete reality contained in the spiritual conception of the world be grasped.

Naturally, these influences from the spiritual world are not at work in the case of children only; influences also come from individualities in the spiritual world who were connected with human beings at a later age of life. To begin with, an individual may be quite unaware of these influences. (Again, I am not inventing but telling you of actual observations, confirmed by spiritual investigation.) After a time, he may say to himself: "I do not know why I am impelled to this or that action, why I have this impulse; something is urging me to think quite differently now about certain things." Subsequently, he may have a very striking dream. Little heed is paid to things of the kind nowadays, but people will gradually become aware that it is not the "form" but the content of the dream that is of importance. From this you may conclude that if Edison had made his discoveries in a dream, they would have been just as effective! Suppose someone dreams that an unknown person comes to him, a person he cannot even think of as an acquaintance, indeed cannot place at all. This person comes into his life of dream and various things happen. Finally, he realizes that this person whom he cannot recall, who died perhaps fifteen years before, is working into and influencing his life. Whereas previously he felt that certain impulses were urging him on, he is now fully aware that these impulses, in the form of a dream-picture, are working into his night-consciousness. This is often characteristic of the connection between impulses within us and influences working upon us in the shape of dreams. Such experiences will become increasingly familiar.

And now, in conclusion, let us see how they will become familiar.

Suppose someone today reads one of the many biographies of Raphael. He will get the impression that in a certain respect Raphael stands there as a phenomenon, complete in himself, giving forth the highest and best that was in him, but so enclosed within his particular sphere of work that it is difficult to imagine him rising still higher or transcending the level he had actually reached. And again: Raphael's creative genius seems to have been alive in him from the very beginning. On the subject of its phenomenal manifestation in Raphael's early boyhood the biographies have nothing to say. And why?

The biographies give the information that Raphael's father was Giovanni Santi,[†] who, among other activities, was also a writer; he died when Raphael was eleven years old, but before his death he had placed the boy under the tuition of a painter. It is also known that Giovanni Santi was himself a talented painter but that there was something in him which he could not bring to expression. We feel that there was something in the soul of Giovanni Santi which did not make itself manifest because his outer nature frustrated it. He died when the boy Raphael was eleven years old. From the very way in which Raphael develops, we can discern the source of the powers which enabled him to reach maturity and perfection so rapidl—they are the influences playing into him from his father, forces coming from the spiritual worlds. Anyone who tries to write a true biography of Raphael in the future will have to emphasize the point that Giovanni Santi, the father of Raphael, died in 1494, when the boy was only eleven years old. Giovanni Santi was a distinguished man, who during his life on Earth aspired to great things. And his aspirations continued when, living on without frustration in the spiritual world, he was sending down to his beloved son—in the form of delicate and intimate spiritual influences—forces which his own constitution had prevented him from bringing to expression in the physical world.

To say this is no disparagement of Raphael's genius, for the ground must naturally have been there. We know that he was the reincarnation of John the Baptist and had only to receive into himself those forces which it was his particular mission to bring into manifestation at that time. Thinking of this, we can perceive the interplay between the spiritual world and the physical plane. Future study of the life of Raphael will have, at every turn, to concern itself with the influences which poured from the spiritual into the physical. Then we shall have a picture of "wholeness"—of forces working around us, through us, in us. Thus will spirituality again be instilled into culture. But it must not surprise us if those who are unwilling today to listen to any suggestion of the introduction of spirituality into culture are contemptuous of this spiritual conception of the world; for it is something completely new. It is a dawning of the new power of the spirit self. And a time will come—I ask you to write this deeply into your souls—when human beings will think of the materialistic culture which is now on the way to its close, as they once thought about the age preceding the Flood, yearning and longing for the future culture which, when it came, was something wholly and essentially new. Theosophists, however, should not merely strive for this ideal in theory, but receive it into their very souls; they should regard it as their good karma to know about the course of human evolution and therewith of human culture.

These things will have to be pondered over for a time, because I am not yet in a position to say exactly when the next lecture can take place. But we know well that time is required to make spiritual science an integral force and impulse in our hearts and minds; and we know, too, that it is part of spiritual development not only to understand the truths but actually to unfold all that the great ideas born from a spiritual conception of the world can say to our hearts.

Lecture Eight

BERLIN, JUNE 18, 1912

It will be my task today to speak of the nature and being of man, in order that the next lecture may contribute to an understanding of the development of mankind as a whole.

We will begin by considering something of primary and immediate importance in the life of the human being as he stands before us on the Earth. You know, of course, that the human being, as we see him, is not the creation of the Earth alone, but that his origin must be traced back to much earlier conditions of existence. From many writings and lectures you know that through spiritual-scientific research these preceding conditions of evolution, the preceding embodiments of the planet Earth, can be discovered and appropriately known as the pre-earthly Saturn condition, the pre-earthly Sun condition, and the pre-earthly Moon condition of our planet. The forces in man as a whole being do not proceed merely from processes that have been in operation on the Earth; the being of man contains heritages, as it were, from the earlier planetary conditions. These heritages have remained and are active in man. The human being in his whole nature can be understood only when we know that the first foundations of the physical body were laid during the ancient Saturn period; development proceeded through the Old Sun period and the Old Moon period, and the present form and structure of the human body did not unfold until the period of Earth evolution proper. In the other principles of human nature, too, heritages of pre-earthly conditions, not merely forces originating on the Earth, are actively in operation. Today, however, we will think of what man is as a creation of the Earth, living out his existence on the Earth; we will think of what is incorporated in his being during the Earth period, in pursuance of the mission of the Earth.

The powers or principles derived specifically from the Earth can be differentiated into three. There is, firstly, man's earthly *consciousness*; it is derived from the Earth and the forces of the Earth. It is, of all principles, the one that is most immediately present in the human being as he moves about the world today; and the purpose of everything that has come to pass in the process of the Earth's evolution has been to enable the human being, here on the Earth, to unfold his present consciousness. Consciousness is the most intensely present, the most familiar reality; it pervades and fills all waking existence; in it your thoughts, perceptions, feelings, and impulses of will run their course, in so far as you are "awake" human beings. This consciousness you know so well was not possessed by man in the pre-earthly conditions of the Earth, nor indeed during the first period of Earth evolution proper—which, to begin with, was only a recapitulation of pre-earthly conditions. Man acquired it gradually; or rather, it was bestowed upon him by the creative powers and forces of the cosmos.

In order to possess this consciousness, the human being must waken from sleep and must make use of the senses, that is to say, of the instruments of the body. That he must also make use of instruments other than the senses is obvious; for in this everyday waking consciousness, he does not merely formulate ideas and thoughts but also has feelings, experiences, impulses of will. This whole content of consciousness, filling and forming it, needs the outer, physical body, the earthly body; when an idea or thought is formed, the soul-spiritual being makes use of the instrument of the physical body. From this it is easy to realize that the consciousness into which the human being wakens in the morning is dependent upon the earthly body, and that when he thinks, feels or wills in this ordinary consciousness, he can only do so because he has the physical earthly body as an instrument.

As you will have read in the book *Occult Science*,[†] the states of consciousness between death and a new birth are essentially different from those of consciousness as it is on Earth. For consciousness changes according to its instrument, and between death and rebirth, as a being of soul and spirit, man has at his disposal instruments of a different character from those available to him during life in the physical body. The physical body, from which the instruments of everyday consciousness are formed, disintegrates and decays at death. Or rather, in the sense of spiritual science it would be better, instead of using the word "decay," to say that it is given over to the element of universal nature, for the dissolution or decay of the physical body observed outwardly is only illusion, *maya*. In reality, a great and mighty process underlies what is called the "dissolution" or "decay" of the human body. Whatever in man belongs to nature passes over to powers standing behind existence. At death, the physical body of earthly man slips away, falls away from him; so that in speaking of man as a being of the Earth, we can only say that the instrument of his everyday consciousness falls away from him at death.

Here we have the first principle of Earthly man: his *consciousness*. In considering his whole being, however, something must be kept separate and distinct from what is known as "consciousness" *per se* in ordinary sense existence—something that is not, in the same sense as thinking, feeling, and willing, to be included in the general sphere of consciousness. What we call *memory* is distinct from these other processes. The thoughts and feelings arising from the store of memory and of remembrances are not subject to the same laws as the consciousness of which we have here been speaking. In order that consciousness may exist at all, the physical body must be preserved in its accustomed form. In respect of its "substance," the physical body is being renewed all the time; after seven or eight years, we have within us quite other physical substances than were previously there. The physical substances change, but the "form" remains. And the form must remain, for it is the instrument for the ordinary consciousness. Ordinary consciousness can unfold thinking, feeling, and willing during the time the physical body retains its form. If, however, memory and remembrances were bound up with the "physical body," they would not be able to survive for very long—at most for as long as the various substances of the physical body remain. This means that if memory were bound up with the physical body, we should be able, at most, to remember back six or seven years. The physical body is not, however, the instrument of memory; in earthly man, the instrument of memory is the etheric body, or life body. The etheric body is actively in operation through the whole life of man on Earth—so that what has been taken into the memory, from the first moment of consciousness to death, can remain all the time. It is this etheric or life body which carries remembrances, memory pictures, from one period in life across to the other. The instrument for earthly consciousness, therefore, is the physical body; the instrument for memory and remembrance is the etheric body. We would not be able to carry the remembrances of our life across the period stretching between death and a new birth if something quite definite did not take place—if, after forsaking the physical body at death, we did not remain for a certain space of time in the etheric or life body. This is the interval after death during which the past life spreads out like a great panorama, a great tableau. This "life tableau" can only appear to us because after death we retain the etheric body for a short time. The etheric body is the instrument for acts of remembrance or recollection and if we were to lose it altogether at death or immediately afterwards, no such tableau could rise up before us. We must be able to use the etheric body as an instrument, and something takes place while this life-tableau is before us after death. This whole life tableau is gathered, "inscribed," as it were, into the universal life ether permeating space. And there it remains—in the universal life ether. What was retained at the beginning for a few days only is now inscribed in the universal life ether in which we live perpetually. Because it is thus inscribed, it is present throughout our further existence between death and the new birth in the future. We take with us through that period an "extract" of our etheric body, so that a connection can always be established with the life-tableau that has been inscribed into the universal life ether. This is a kind of permanent organ whereby the remembrances of the last life remain accessible.

In consciousness *per se* there is, and can only be, the immediate present; the immediate reality of "being" would vanish with the passing moment if, as people of Earth, we could only unfold consciousness in acts of thinking, feeling, and willing. That we are able to *preserve* what is contained in our life of thinking, of feeling, and of will is due to the etheric body; and even after death it is still preserved, in the universal life ether. There we have the second principle of earthly, human existence: that which does not take flight with the passing moment but remains in existence, preserved in the universal life ether. Thus, in the man of Earth, two principles are to be specified: earthly consciousness, and memory or remembrances—which are not to be identified with consciousness as such. What, then, is the third principle?

The second principle is distinct from the first in that it does not permit experiences simply to pass away, but preserves them. The third principle of earthly man differs in an important respect from the second. In so far as thoughts have become memories, they have a definite character. Everything that is entrusted to the memory has this characteristic: during your life it is your own, personal possession, part of your own, personal "estate." Memories that go with you through life until the time of death are your innermost possession, a possession remaining in you as a personality until your death. It will not be difficult to realize that what you carry with you through life in your memory, in your remembrances, really means nothing in the outer world. It is within you, and only after death does it begin to mean something in the outer world—when it is inscribed into the universal life ether. In the universal life ether, it is the "registered mark" of your personality. It was inner experience during life, and after death it remains for the following period of eternity as the register of your personality. There it is—inscribed into the life ether. The "inner" during life becomes the "outer" in the life ether after death. Up to the time of death, these memories and remembrances are carried within us as our own, inner possession, and from death onwards they are inscribed like an open secret, as it were, in the life ether; there they live and we remain connected with them because an "extract" from the life body goes with us and we can always look back to what we once experienced. Just as memories and remembrances remain within us during earthly life, so, after death, we are in the life ether, together with the experiences of our past earthly life.

It is different with all that even during our lifetime became *outward* reality—not remaining inward as did the remembrances and memories. Truth to tell, every single step we take with our feet during earthly life becomes outer fact, outer reality; for not only are we able to remember it, but the very step registers our "mark" upon the earthly realm—in that we move through the air, for one thing. Even in the physical sense, the whole of our active life becomes outer reality. And to what a still greater extent is this true of the moral life!

Good and kind-hearted actions in very truth become outer reality. Deeds born of compassion or of sympathy with the joys of our fellow human beings do not live on only within us but also in the other human being, in our whole environment. All the time, the marks and traces of our life are being impressed upon Earth existence. The man for whom we performed a deed of compassion, or a deed born of fellow-feeling with his joy or suffering, carries the influence and effect of our action on with him through life. What we have felt and done lives on in the others, in the outside world. Think about this, and it will soon become plain that such actions do not belong exclusively to the man who performs them in the sense that his memory-pictures belong to him, but they pass over into the world outside as active influences.

What is imparted in this way to the outer world during a person's lifetime is not, like his memory-pictures, inscribed in the etheric body. The etheric body is too intimately and fundamentally part of the whole personality to enable these actions and the effects of them to be registered in it. Nor would this be for the good during earthly life. For if some unkind or mischievous deed, for instance, were immediately to be inscribed in the etheric body, the man would be doomed, throughout his whole life, to be aware of it; it would be a force in his etheric body and in certain circumstances suffering would be entailed; working its way into his life-forces, the bad action would make him ill, discontented, feeble. If acts were inscribed in the etheric body, as are the remembered thoughts, life would be made impossible for earthly man. Just as the etheric body is the instrument for the thoughts, in so far as they become remembrances and memories, so is the astral body the instrument for deeds. Deeds proceed from the astral body. The astral body is the instrument for every action—as I have said, an action becomes part of and works as an influence in the outer world. Everyday consciousness is bound up with the physical body; remembrances and memory with the etheric body; delicate and rarified though the astral body is, every action, remaining as it does as an influence in the outer world, has its source in the astral body. The consequence of this is that actions remain in a certain sense bound up with the astral body, just as memory remains with the etheric body. While the human being is still living in the etheric body after death, the "tableau of memory" unfolds—the memories of the life that is just over remain in the etheric body. When the etheric body has been laid aside after death and all that has been preserved in the form of personal memories has been inscribed into the universal life ether, man's life continues, but now wholly in the astral body. In the astral body he has to live for a long time, bound up with the outer effects caused by his life. After death the human being lives through his actions in backward sequence; he lives backwards through everything he has done to other beings on the earth. For a period amounting approximately to a third of the time of his life, he is living in his astral body through all the actions he performed on Earth. And just as the personal memories are inscribed into the universal life ether when the etheric body is laid aside a few days after death, so in the period during which the human being is bound up with the astral body, all his deeds are inscribed into the all-pervading cosmic astrality. They are within the cosmic astrality and he remains connected with them, just as he is connected with his personal memories which have been recorded as an abiding inscription in the cosmic ether—only his deeds are inscribed, as it were, into a different cosmic register. While the human being is living backwards through the deeds and acts performed in the past life, they are all inscribed in the cosmic astrality and he remains connected with them. Through his astral body, therefore, the earthly man remains connected with his deeds.

What I have just described is *karma*. What has been inscribed into the all-pervading cosmic astrality by a man's deeds—that, in very truth, is karma. That a strong moral stimulus lies in such knowledge is quite obvious, and possible allegations to the effect that spiritual science does not provide the deepest moral basis for life would be malicious calumny.

In what sense may we speak of a strong moral impulse in the principles of knowledge here described? Deeds performed during life are inscribed, after death, into the cosmic astrality. If a person has committed wrongs and has not, to the best of his ability, been able karmically to put them right during life, all such actions are written into his karma and remain connected with him. (Assuming that already in earthly life he did all he could to right some wrong or sinful action, he would thereby be spared from having it inscribed into his karma.) In that as a human being of the Earth he has an earthly astral body, he has his karma.

As a being of the Earth, then, man has, firstly, consciousness, of which the physical body is the instrument; secondly, his memory, with the etheric body or life-body as its instrument; and thirdly, karma—which belongs to him just as consciousness belongs to him in the physical body. In this sense, earthly man is a threefold being, consisting of his *earthly consciousness*, his *memory*, and his *karma*. Without these principles he is not, in the real sense, a man of Earth. A being who went about on Earth without unfolding in his physical body the consciousness belonging to human existence on Earth, would not be man. A being who did not unfold the faculty of memory belonging to human existence on Earth, would not be man. Nor would a being who went through life in an earthly body without creating karma be man. What constitutes the Earth-man is that he unfolds consciousness through the physical body, memory and remembrance through the etheric body, and through the astral body creates karma. These are the "earthly" principles in the being of man. A fourth principle must be added—namely, the I. This is the principle of which we know that it flashed up, for the first time, in Earth existence. The I passes from incarnation to incarnation, is within us while we are unfolding our earthly consciousness, while we are preserving picture after picture in our memory, and while we are accumulating karma from one incarnation to another. The I is within us, within these three principles of earthly man. What, then, still remains to be said about the earthly man?

The I flashed into manifestation for the first time on the *Earth*. The foundations of the physical body of earthly man were laid during the Old Saturn period of evolution. Although after the Old Moon period, Earth evolution changed the nature of the physical body, the physical body is not a product of the Earth proper. The same is to be said of the etheric body—which was laid down in seed form during the Old Sun period—and of the astral body for which the first foundations were laid during the Old Moon period. Let us try to picture the human being the following way. When Earth existence began, man came over from a pre-earthly evolution, as a being consisting of physical body, etheric body and astral body. In the course of Earth evolution, his physical body was transformed into the instrument for his earthly consciousness, his etheric body into the instrument of his personal memory, and his astral body into the bearer of karma. Physical body, etheric body, astral body—these were bestowed upon man by earlier, pre-earthly periods of evolution, after which the Earth, in accordance with its mission, elaborated these three principles of his being. Let us keep them distinct. The physical body of man has become the marvelous, wonderful structure it is because it has passed through three stages of metamorphosis, together with the three earlier embodiments of the planet Earth; if it had remained as it was after the expiration of the Old Moon period, it would have been endowed with all the inner qualities it now possesses but would not have been metamorphosed in such a way as to enable it to become the instrument of consciousness for earthly man. The physical body has not only the perfection it had attained at the end of the Old Moon evolution but, in addition, it has been so transformed as to become the bearer of the earthly consciousness of man. In the same way, the etheric body has all the perfections previously contained within it, but only since the beginning of Earth evolution has it developed the forces which make it the bearer of man's personal memory. The astral body had acquired many perfections during the Old Moon period, but only through the operation of earthly processes could it become the instrument for the creation of karma. The I alone has been equipped with all its powers solely by the Earth. What the Earth itself worked into the being of man is to be observed only in the I. What, then, has really been added to the human being by the I?

Let us suppose that man had all the qualities and attributes which the Earth-mission has instilled into him, but *not* the I. This is, of course, an impossible hypothesis because the I had necessarily to be bestowed upon him. But let us assume that without unfolding the I, a being possessed the earthly qualities contained in physical body, etheric body, astral body. Even if it had not been possible to develop these qualities and attributes on the Earth, their development might have been possible on other planetary bodies, and spiritual science is able to study the conditions of existence prevailing on other planets. A being of this kind would be able to unfold waking consciousness as it exists in man, would possess the faculties of thinking, feeling, and willing, but would not connect his thoughts, experiences, feelings or impulses of will, with an I-consciousness. Nevertheless, it would be possible for such a being to have, like earthly man, consciousness, remembrances, the power to retain ideas and thoughts in the memory, and also karma. Such a condition would not be possible in an earthly man; but let us envisage that there might exist a being of his kind. What would there be within him? Consciousness, memory, karma—as they are within the human being. But in the earthly human being, the I, too, is present. What, then, is brought about by the I? Since karma is created, essentially, by the astral body, how does the I operate within its own sphere of karma?

What is brought about by the I itself is of even greater moment than human karma. For karma remains connected with the human being. Deeds performed in some life persist as his karma, and he can make compensation for them in a later life. In reality, it is the astral body which causes karma to remain. But the I is a spiritual potency, a spiritual being. What the I creates, as the astral body creates karma, does not remain connected with man but detaches itself from him as *forms created by thoughts*. Whereas what is inscribed in his karma remains connected with him and is instilled into subsequent phases of Earth evolution, something else—of a very definite character—is brought into existence by the human I, and passes over into other worlds—as memories pass over into the cosmic life ether. Just as karma is inscribed in the cosmic astrality, so the creations of the I—the forms created by thoughts and feelings—go forth into the world. Karma remains connected with the human being; but there are other creations—creations of the I—which detach themselves from him, to begin with, simply as forms, and live on as spiritual forms in the universe. What, then, is it in the human being that lives on? Firstly, his personal memories; secondly, his karma; thirdly, the forms born of his thoughts and feelings. But whereas he remains connected with his memories and with his karma, these thought-forms detach themselves from him and, as forms, become independent. As lifeless forms—which actually go forth as forms—the creations of our I live on in the outer world.

We will pick up on this point next time and carry our considerations further.

Lecture Nine

BERLIN, JUNE 20, 1912

In the preceding lecture, we studied the principles and powers in the being of man belonging specifically to Earth existence. Certain forces operating in human nature are, in reality, "heritages" from the earlier embodiments of the Earth: from the Old Saturn period, the Old Sun period, and the Old Moon period. These heritages from primeval epochs of evolution are contained in the physical body, the etheric body, and the astral body of the earthly human being; but it is the Earth, the forces deriving actually from the Earth, that have made the physical body into the instrument of man's present form of consciousness. The etheric body has received, specifically from the Earth, the qualities whereby it becomes the bearer of memory, the instrument of remembrance. The astral body itself developed during the Old Moon period of evolution—the planetary predecessor of the Earth—and the Earth adds the forces which provide for the operation of human karma. But something else exists as an activity, an expression of the human personality, something specifically connected with the I in man which has been acquired only during Earth evolution. Waking consciousness, memory and remembrance, the operation of karma—these were the active principles added to the physical, etheric, and astral bodies in that man was endowed with the I. We said that the forces of the I are sent outwards, towards the outer spiritual world, and that these forces, unlike those inhering in karma, or in memory, do not remain inexorably bound up with the human being. A man's memories and remembrances remain part of him; his consciousness, obviously, has significance only for him, for other beings have quite different forms of consciousness; and karma is bound up with the human being in so far as it has to operate during the earthly incarnations to adjust and make compensation for his deeds. But "forms" or "forces" begotten of thoughts or feelings—these detach themselves from the real I of man, and in a certain respect acquire independent existence, independent reality. Unlike the other forces, they do not remain connected with him.

Now, in respect of the forms or forces deriving from the I of man, a sharp distinction must be made. The human I can unfold either selfishness or selflessness in the inner life. According to whether selfishness or selfless love and compassion are unfolded, these "forces" or "forms" operate quite differently. The forces of selfish thoughts become forces of disturbance, even of destruction; they pass into the spiritual world actually as destructive forces. On the other hand, all forces of selfless thoughts enter into the spiritual life of Earth evolution, not as destructive but as upbuilding, constructive forces. In that these forces of selfless thought detach themselves, as it were, from the I of man, they leave behind certain traces in him. Especially is it true of forces begotten of selfless thoughts and feelings that as they go forth from the I, they leave traces behind in the human being—traces which are quite perceptible. The more the I sends out forces born of selfless thoughts and feelings, the more does a person develop individuality of form, of gesture, facial expression, and so on—in short, the power inherent in his own being. The forces of selfish, self-seeking thoughts and feelings, however, work in him in such a way that he has little power to give expression to his own individuality. We must therefore ask: What is the principle underlying the distinction to be made among the individual forms of human beings in the course of the evolution of humanity?

Everything that is "form" on the Earth derives from the Spirits of Form. The name "Spirits of Form" is actually given to these beings of the higher hierarchies because everything that has form, shape, life—everything that takes on shape inwardly and evolves an outer form—has received the essential impetus for this form from the Spirits of Form. Now all these beings of the higher hierarchies are involved in a constant process of evolution. Not only man, but in a certain sense all the beings of the different hierarchies are involved in a constant process of evolution. In our present age, the Spirits of Form are moving to the higher rank of "Spirits of Movement"; the "Spirits of Personality" to that of "Spirits of Form"; the "Archangeloi" to that of "Spirits of Personality" or "Archai." However, as the Spirits of Form move upward in rank and actually lose the character of Spirits of Form, it is *not* the case that the rising Spirits of Personality immediately assume the functions of Spirits of Form. This will help you to understand that something quite definite will come about during the second half of the period of Earth evolution into which we have now passed. At the beginning of Earth evolution, the Spirits of Form stamped the principle of form into man; this comes to expression in the different human forms. Just as the various races have developed their characteristic qualities, and individual human beings take on the traits of the several races, so have the various groups of humanity as a whole all over the Earth received their stamp from the Spirits of Form. What the Spirits of Form stamped into human beings has long since passed into the processes of heredity; it has long since become a heritage, handed down from generation to generation. In a sense, the Spirits of Form leave man greater freedom as they themselves move into a higher category and withdraw from the form-creating function that devolved upon them at the beginning of Earth evolution. So far as the beings of the hierarchies are concerned, man is drawing nearer and nearer to his "coming of age." But of this we must be clear: the spiritual beings, moving up as they do to higher ranks, must also evolve and prepare for the next planetary condition of the Earth, in order that during the Jupiter existence, they may endow the beings who once belonged to the Earth with forms which will then be appropriate. Towards the end of a planetary age, it is always the case that the being of central importance—and on the Earth this is *man*—is left free, so that the qualities with which he was originally endowed may pass more freely into his own hands. In the course of Earth evolution in the future, therefore, the forces of form, the forms begotten by thoughts and feelings, will assume greater and greater importance. And in so far as they are selfless, in so far as they are the offspring of selfless wisdom, selfless love, these forces will work formatively upon man. For the design or pattern of the evolutionary process may be indicated in the following way. The further we go back into the past, the more do we find that the outer form of the child resembles that of its forefathers; but the further we go into the future, the more will the human being, in his outward appearance, become an expression of the *individuality* who passes on from one incarnation to another. This means that in one and the same family (even now it is very frequently the case and nobody with an eye for such things will deny it), there will be less and less likeness between the faces of the children and between the faces of the children and between the other parts of the human figure, for the forms will no longer be the expression of family or race but more and more the expression of the individuality. Anyone with a knowledge of spiritual science, if he really observes human beings living all over the Earth, can perceive, even today, side by side with the inherited characteristics of race or family, more and more strongly individual lineaments of face, head, and other bodily forms; he can perceive the striking differences in form and figure among members of one and the same family. In this respect, of course, we are in a period of transition; but the sixth post-Atlantean epoch is in preparation, together with its paramount characteristic—namely, that unlike the conditions obtaining in earlier periods of culture, outer marks of race will be much less of a criterion. In the sixth epoch, the criterion all over the Earth will be the extent to which the individuality has impressed upon his countenance and upon the whole of his being, the forces left behind by the forms begotten of selfless thoughts and feelings—especially those deriving from wisdom.

It is contrary to every principle of true spiritual science to say that just as there was one leading race in each of the culture-epochs in the past, so in the future, too, there will be another such race, distinguished by physical attributes. The ancient Indian culture was borne and sustained by a leading race; so, too, was the culture of ancient Persia, of the Egypto-Chaldean and Greco-Latin epochs. But already today it is apparent that culture, instead of being borne by one specific leading race, spreads over all races. And it is by spiritual science that culture—a spiritual culture—must be carried over the whole Earth, without distinction of race or blood. It is already apparent that our epoch will be succeeded by another of quite a different character, an epoch when, all over the Earth, the extent to which a man expresses his innermost being in his outer form will be made manifest. It would be sheer contradiction of every principle of spiritual science to speak today of continental limits, or the limits of any particular territory, in connection with human beings belonging to the sixth epoch of culture—for they, in the future, will be spread over the whole Earth. Only someone whose vantage-point is not that of spiritual science but who has some strange contradictory idea that a kind of wheel revolving in spiritual evolution causes everything to repeat itself, just as spring, summer, autumn, and winter repeat themselves when a year has run its course—only such a person could make the statement that what was necessary for the creation of races in earlier times will simply be repeated for the sixth epoch. Such a statement would be entirely at variance with true spiritual science, and would cut across all knowledge of the actual and real progress of humanity. The inner power of the soul becomes more and more manifest as evolution goes forward. The old is not repeated merely in slightly different form, but actual progress takes place in the evolution of humanity. If theosophy is to keep faith with its good old principles—the first of which is to promote culture without distinction of race, color, and so forth, it will not cherish groundless hopes of a future culture emanating from one particular race. The deeper connection of theosophy with the actual course of evolution consists precisely in this: that the processes operating in world evolution are understood, that thinking and feeling are brought into harmony with theosophical knowledge and the necessary impulses of will made effective in the world. In order to understand how the power of the soul will more and more be made manifest in humanity, it is only necessary to bring out one point clearly, and then we shall realize how the human being evolves as an individual. (The point that has been developed today has been dealt with repeatedly, for many years.)

At the beginning of Earth evolution, the human being was part of a group soul—as expressed in race, blood, family and so on—to a far greater extent than was the case later on. As evolution continues, he becomes more and more of an *individual*, develops his individuality. We have heard what an important part certain forces play in the development of the individuality during Earth evolution: consciousness that is dependent on the physical body; memory and remembrance which are dependent upon the etheric body; and karma, whereby a man can make real progress, in that his imperfections and faults do not remain but can be overcome by him as he passes through one incarnation after another. But the "forms" or "forces" created by thoughts and feelings, although they detach themselves from the human being and lead an independent existence, are nevertheless closely united with him, in that they leave vestiges behind; these vestiges, as they are sent out by the I, contribute to the definition of the individuality, and man gradually divests himself of the qualities belonging to the group soul. The trend which will become more and more general over the globe and will form the essential, fundamental character of the sixth epoch of culture is no kind of approach to a new group soul, but far rather the laying aside of the attributes of the group soul. Intimately connected with this is the fact that the spiritual guidance of human beings will become more and more a matter individual to each one; they will have greater inner freedom in this respect.

Anyone who has understood the trend of the little book *The Spiritual Guidance of the Individual and Humanity*[†] will realize that a movement in this direction is in very truth taking place in the human race. It is a fact that in ancient times people lived under external leaders and teachers, but even in those days, leadership was gradually becoming an inner concern. Just as the outer form becomes an expression of the individuality, so does the path to the spiritual worlds taken by human beings become more and more their individual concern. It is the duty of those who have insight into the signs of the times to insist that human beings have not remained stationary at an earlier stage of development, that the forces once employed, cannot be repeated in the same form, simply because humanity has gone forward in its evolution. In the age that is coming, human souls will become more and more mature, able to discern and perceive those things of which spiritual science teaches today.

The Mystery of Golgotha, as the essential Christ-event, was an outer happening, striking into the physical world; a future Christ-event will be an *inner* concern, inasmuch as the soul of man has been so quickened by the first Christ-event that in days to come, the way to Christ will be found in the spirit, out of the life of soul.

Wherever you look in spiritual science as it is presented here, you will always find—even in the case of very specialized details—that it is consistent with your own powers of reason and free judgment, provided only that you make a real effort to apply this free power of judgment. In that the individual human being is all the time becoming more accessible to influences from the spiritual world, the authority of external leadership will gradually lose its weight. It is very important to realize that the ancient wisdom exists and must be understood, that understanding of it can constantly increase if human souls are open to the spiritual worlds and if they strive to grasp this wisdom with their powers of reason. This is the very essence of progressive evolution. However specialized the subjects may be, appeal to individual reason and judgment must never be excluded. It is a very different thing to bring forward some young man and announce that he has this and that incarnation behind him! If I were to tell you such things I should beg you at the outset not to believe them simply on my word—but I should never dream of making such assertions authoritatively, for the simple reason that you could not possibly convince yourselves objectively of their truth. When, however, it is said that the same individuality was present in Elijah, John the Baptist, Raphael, and Novalis—all long since dead—you can yourselves discover by studying their lives, whether there are reasonable and sound grounds for such a statement. And no other kind of appeal must ever be made; the respect due to each individual soul demands that such a test should be within the realm of possibility. There are, of course, lazy-minded people who say: "We have to 'believe' you when you speak of the same individuality having lived in Elijah, John the Baptist, Raphael, and Novalis." No! They are not obliged to believe it, but they can try, at least, to find evidence in the different lives of what, admittedly, can only be actually discovered by occult research. This evidence can be found, and it is pure laziness when people say that if someone speaks of the incarnations of human beings long since dead, this must be taken on authority just as is the case when the incarnations of some young person living today are announced.

That is a very different matter! In this respect, a deep appeal must be made to theosophists to put everything to the test of reason and not to rest content with the cheap excuse that things cannot be proved. They can be proved, if there is willingness to do so. This must be constantly emphasized.

A kind of counterbalancing process operates in the world, and while, on the one hand, the development of the individuality is progressing, on the other, something else will become more and more universal—namely, the *objective knowledge* which must be acquired by man. Objectivity of knowledge, uniformity of knowledge does not gainsay the principle of individuality. Mathematics in itself is an illustration of this fact. And so it is the task of occultism—if one may speak of occultism having such a task at the present time—to provide objective wisdom and knowledge of the universe. Even though, in the nature of things, the ideal is not immediately in sight because not every individual has sufficient time and opportunity to put specific details to the test, it is true, nevertheless, that although things can actually be discovered only through occult research, they can be examined and endorsed by every individual; it is *not* necessary to take them on faith. All that is required is to reflect about things, with reason and sound judgment. Let us take a definite case, remembering that what will be said about it is applicable everywhere.

Suppose someone says: "Mankind has evolved. Progress is a reality in evolution. This progress reveals itself in the fact that man is becoming more strongly individual in his nature and being. It follows that whereas in olden times, leadership was vested more in persons, in times to come this kind of leadership will be superseded by objective wisdom, objective knowledge; personal leadership will recede and become merely an instrument and means for bringing objective wisdom to the human being. The ideal vantage-point is that the occult teacher is no different from a teacher of mathematics, who quite obviously has his function. But mathematics are not accepted merely on the authority of the teacher of mathematics; every individual accepts mathematics because he gradually acquires knowledge and understanding of the fundamentals. Hence the element of wisdom and of knowledge will more and more supersede the element of personality."

Suppose that such a statement were confronted by another, to the effect that "the world rolls onwards like a wheel; in olden days there were great teachers of humanity, and new ones are about to come." When faced with a statement like that, it is not possible to adopt the easy-going principle that either the one or the other may be believed; it is a matter, then, for deciding: which of the two is acceptable to reason? There is the choice between deciding whether no progress is to be ascribed to humanity and everything thought of as eternal repetition, or whether humanity does really progress and that evolution has meaning and purpose. Those who refuse to recognize any meaning in evolution can speak, if they like, of the eternal repetition of epochs of time; but those who see meaning and purpose in Earth existence as brought to light by occult research will not speak of eternal repetition of the same things—which does not, in fact, take place.

It is all-important to realize that the faculties of man have *developed* and that in this development—to take one example—the following is involved. In the ancient mysteries, each human being was obliged to submit to certain enactments and procedures directed to his own person; thereby he became an initiate. He passed through the different grades of initiation. In and through the Mystery of Golgotha, these grades of initiation became a world-historical event, made manifest for all humanity. What had in olden times been an affair of one or another particular center of initiation became a world-historical event, passed into the common estate of humanity, and was thereafter accessible to every advancing individuality. In my book *Christianity as Mystical Fact*,[†] therefore, the Mystery of Golgotha is described as the culmination and, in a sense, the close of the ancient mysteries, because it brought all the ancient religions into one great unity. Occultism reveals still more clearly how the several streams of culture are gradually converging into one; but as they converge, they must be recognized and identified. The very operations of occult research reveal how the fruits of this research harmonize with what everyone can accept for himself, from his own observation of happenings on the physical plane.

Let us take a very far-reaching example, of which you may well say, to begin with: "There he is telling us something that really cannot be put to the test of reason, nor even approached by reason." You may well say this, when it is first put before you.

My book *An Outline of Occult Science* describes how, at one time, Sun, Moon, and Earth were united in a single planetary existence; the Sun then separated off and, at a later stage, Mercury and Venus; still later, Mars separated off from the Sun. The further we go back in time, the more does such a process become a spiritual process and the question it is essential to understand is really this: Who were the *beings* who thus separated? Of primary importance as regards the Earth was the Christ-being, the great Sun being who through the Mystery of Golgotha subsequently united again with the Earth. Thereby all the antecedents of Christianity were brought to a kind of climax and culmination in Christianity itself. With the Mystery of Golgotha, a mighty cosmic power streamed into Earth evolution. It might conceivably be argued that if the Christ came once and once only, this would imply injustice to the souls who lived before his coming. If a materialist were to bring forward such an argument, it might be understandable, but it would certainly not be understandable if it came from a theosophist. For he knows that the souls living today also lived in earlier times, before the Mystery of Golgotha; the coming of Christ, therefore, is of equal significance for the souls of the pre-Christian ages, because they all incarnate again in the times following the Mystery of Golgotha. There is, however, this point to be made and it must be understood by theosophists—namely, that in a certain sense the Buddha forms an exception. We must reach the vantage-point of the true Buddhist who says that the individuality in the Buddha was that of a Bodhisattva who was born as the son of King Suddhodana, rose in his twenty-ninth year to the rank of Buddha, thereby attaining a height whence he need no longer return to a body of flesh. That, therefore, was the final incarnation of the Bodhisattva individuality who does not reincarnate in the era following the founding of Christianity. In Christiania—in the lectures "Man in the Light of Occultism, Theosophy, and Philosophy,"[†] in June 1912—I drew attention to the fact that a very special mission in the universe devolves upon an individuality as sublime as the Buddha. The individuality who became the Buddha had been sent from the hosts of

Christ on the Sun to the "Venus men" before they came to the Earth (see also the description in *Occult Science*); the individuality of the Buddha, therefore, had been sent forth by Christ from the Sun to Venus, as His emissary. This individuality came to the Earth with the "Venus men" and had thus reached such an advanced stage of development that through the Atlantean, on into the post-Atlantean era, he was able to attain to the rank of Buddhahood before the coming of Christ. He was in very truth a "Christian" before the time of Christ. We know, too, that later on he revealed himself in the astral body of the Jesus child of Luke's Gospel—since he need no longer return in a body of flesh. United as he is with the Christ-stream, a different task devolves upon him for the times to come. (This task was described in greater detail in the Christiania lectures.) The Buddha need not incarnate again in a body of flesh. It fell to him to fulfil a certain deed on Mars—a deed not identical with the Mystery of Golgotha but to be thought of as a parallel—namely, the redemption of the people of Mars. There is, of course, no question here of a Crucifixion as in the Mystery of Golgotha, for as may be read in *Occult Science*, the people of Mars are quite differently constituted from human beings on Earth. These things, of course, are the results of occult observation and can only be discovered through clairvoyant investigation.

Now let us think of this fact—that the Buddha was an emissary of the Christ and had lived on Venus. Then think of the uniqueness of the Buddha life, of its fundamental character, and proceed as I did myself. First, there came to me the occult knowledge: Buddha goes from Venus to Mars in order there to accomplish a deed of redemption for the beings of Mars. And now take the life of Buddha, and observe how strikingly it differs from the lives of all the other founders of religion in that period. The teachings of all the others tend in the direction of concealing the doctrine of reincarnation; Buddha teaches reincarnation and founds a community based essentially upon piety, upon a kind of remoteness from the world. Ask yourselves whether there are beings for whom this quality would be of fundamental significance—beings whose redemption could be wrought by all that the Buddha had lived through and made his own. If it were possible, now, to say more about the constitution of the Mars beings, you would see that the Buddha life was a kind of preparation for a higher mission, that it occurred in Earth existence as a kind of culmination and can have no direct continuation. You may compare much in the Buddha life with the indications given by occultism and then you will be able to form some real judgment of matters with such far-reaching cosmic connections. To discover them—that will still be beyond you; but you will be able to examine and study them with the help of all the material at your disposal, and you will find agreement and conformity among the indications given. That Buddha is connected with Venus was known, also, to H. P. Blavatsky.† In her *Secret Doctrine*, she writes: "Buddha = Mercury." "Mercury" because in earlier times the names for Venus and Mercury were confused and reversed. "Buddha = Venus" would be the proper form. A knowledge possessed by occultists today is already hinted at in H. P. Blavatsky's *Secret Doctrine*—but it must be understood correctly.

These things are connected with the whole process of advancing evolution. The evolution of man must be studied in connection with the whole universe; man must be thought of as a microcosm within the macrocosm. The fact that beings do actually mediate between the several planets is entirely in line with these concatenations of cosmic existence, so that a being like the Buddha can actually be regarded as a mediator between planets. A good principle on which judgment of all these things may be based is recognition of human progress as a reality, recognition of "evolution," not as a catchword but as a truth.

How can we fail to realize that evolution is a reality? Goethe has shown with such beauty that in each plant, green leaf, petal, calyx, stamen, and pistil are a unity, and yet progress is clearly to be observed—from the green leaf to the petal and the fruit. Progress in the spiritual life is still more clearly perceptible. It would be pure abstraction to say that the path of the mystic has everywhere been the same, among all peoples and in all ages. If one were content with cheap persuasion, it would be quite easy to tell people that the mystical experience of a yogi has never differed from that of a Christian saint. But such a statement would not be based upon knowledge of the facts—not even of the external facts. The experiences of a yogi and those of a Christian Mystic like St. Theresa, for example, differ fundamentally and essentially! Is it not casting all sense of truth to the winds to compare the experience of an Indian yogi with experiences that are permeated through and through with the Christ-principle—or with the Jesus-principle in the case of St. Theresa? As true as there is a difference between the red petal of the rose and the green leaf on its stalk, so is it true that there is a difference between experiences arising in the practice of yoga and those of a later age. There is a fundamental difference and a progression as well. Even if many lapses occur, it can be perceived, nevertheless, and the progress outruns and overcomes the lapses.

It is possible for everyone to put these principles to the test of reason—and that is essential. For theosophy must be given under the assumption that it speaks to the innermost soul, the innermost heart, but is also grasped and assimilated. It would imply that human beings could never come of age if in the future they were obliged to wait, in the same way as was necessary in olden times, for the coming of "world teachers"—and this quite apart from the fact that no true occultism will ever speak of such an abstract principle of repetition, because it is a direct contradiction of what actually happens. As world evolution progresses, the factor of independent judgment and examination will assume greater and greater importance. That is one of the reasons why it is so difficult in the present age to speak truly of an individuality who is so misunderstood, even among occultists—I mean the individuality known as Christian Rosenkreutz. Those who have a real link with him will never disobey the principle here described. But recognition of the principle of evolution—which reveals itself most clearly in the intrinsic worth of a human being—is difficult and gradual. Christian Rosenkreutz, whom we recognize as the one by whom the true occult movement will be led on into the future and who will assuredly never add weight to his authority by means of any outer cult, will be misunderstood—he more than all. Those who have any knowledge of this individuality know, too, that Christian Rosenkreutz will be the greatest of martyrs among men—apart from the Christ who suffered as a god. The martyrdom of Christian Rosenkreutz will be caused by the fact that so few make the resolve to look into their own souls, in order there to seek for the evolving individuality, or to submit to the uncomfortable fact that truth will not be presented ready-made but has to be acquired by intense struggle and effort; requirements of a different character will never be brought forward in the name of the individuality known as Christian Rosenkreutz. These requirements are in line with the character of the present age and with what is felt by people of the present age, even if in many respects they misinterpret it. The present age feels quite distinctly that the principle of individuality will assume greater and greater prominence. Even if here and there this truth is expressed grotesquely and sometimes far too radically, the very fact that it is expressed is indication of a sound instinct in humanity. Many a time one is amazed that in spite of the materialism and the many absurdities current in modern civilization, an absolutely true instinct, although it is often pushed to extremes and caricatured, prevails in regard to many things.

An example occurs in a book recently published: *Zur Kritik der Zeit* [Toward a critique of the age], by Walter Rathenau.[†] It contains a passage to the effect that the time for the founding of sects, for belief in authority, has gone forever as a possible ideal for mankind. As, however, it is a fact that every sound development in our time calls forth its opposite, belief in authority and mania for dogma are rampant in certain circles. And yet, anyone who knows the world today will realize that nothing can so deeply undermine peace and harmony among men as non-recognition of the principle here outlined. The ideal of man must be to fathom and recognize objective truth, to be led through objective truth itself into the spiritual worlds. Hindrances would be laid in his path by attempts to base some truth upon narrow, personal authority—a mode of procedure that is, furthermore, quite impermissible so far as the future is concerned. This must be clearly understood. Many years of work in the field of spiritual science have shown how very difficult things are. Not only here, but wherever theosophical work is possible, it is always difficult to make this principle of theosophical striving the root-nerve of theosophical activity. The reason of the difficulty is that there are always people who will not bestir themselves to grasp what must be the fundamental impulse of our age. Objections that may crop up here and there would die a natural death if people would only give a little thought to the fundamental requirements of the times and realize that humanity is ever and everywhere going forward. To lay hold of the whole essence and spirit of theosophy—that is what matters! But it would run counter to the very essence of theosophy if a certain teaching that is being broadcast today were to find any widespread acceptance—namely, that culture which should be the common property of all mankind without distinction of race and color, is conditioned by some particular continental factor. Is it really possible to take back with one sentence what has been proclaimed in another? Is it difficult to see the contradiction when it is said, on the one hand, that universal wisdom must be spread as a possession of all human beings without distinction of race and other differences, while, on the other, it is said that the civilization of the future rests with a race localized within geographical boundaries? It is high time to reflect on these things and get to the root of them. Is it possible to speak of the progress of humanity when it is constantly reiterated that the same need—in this case, the authority of a personal teacher—exists in the world as of yore? Is it possible to say that man's own spiritual forces must grow stronger, that he must by his own efforts find the way to the spiritual world, if this is made dependent upon the authority of a single individual on the physical Earth? It is extremely easy to say that all opinions have equal weight in the theosophical movement. This remains a catchword when it is not taken really in earnest. Above all it remains a catchword when the opinions of others are misrepresented. Once before I have been obliged to say that "equal right of opinion" is no more than a phrase if our work here—which has nothing whatever to do with any specific territory or race on the Earth—is presented by the other side as though it were suitable only for the German mind. It is an affair of *humanity*, like mathematics—not the affair of any particular nation. To speak of our work here as being an affair of one particular nation, of a strictly limited territory, is an untruth. To quote a catchword does not justify the spreading of untruths in the world. In such circumstances, moreover, the other side may well become the victim of injustice. A semblance of intolerance may easily be created, simply because a stand has to be taken for the truth. The hour shows signs of becoming very serious in this connection.

What I am saying here will be understood only by those who take theosophy in real earnest and will not countenance things that run counter to the fundamental principles of theosophical work. Suppose one were obliged to ward off certain untruths from those who cannot put everything to the test for themselves, can the other person say: "That is intolerance"? He can, of course, say so if, under the guise of truth, he is merely seeking domination and authority! In the future, spiritual truth will work by reason of its own inherent strength, its own power, independently of physical circumstances. And it will be a great and splendid achievement if theosophy can promote unity of culture over the whole Earth. Not for personal reasons, not for national reasons, nor for any "human" reasons whatever, but for purely theosophical reasons it makes one's heart bleed that in England today the President of the Theosophical Society should be making speeches which really cannot be described as "theosophical" but are eminently political. Thinking of the good old traditions of theosophy, the heart bleeds to hear it said in a theosophical address that the day will come for proclaiming: "England together with India, at the center; America and Germany, right and left. One World Policy under the banner of theosophy!" And then we are accused of "intolerance" when it is necessary to protest against the introduction of the personal element into the leadership—where it should never be. It makes an occultist's heart ache that the label "theosophical" should be tacked on to this kind of statement. Once again, I repeat: the heartache is not caused by personal or human considerations but for purely theosophical and occult reasons. It is grievous that the root-principle of theosophical teaching should be tainted—either consciously or unconsciously—with national and imperialistic aspirations! It is grievous to me not because I have anything whatever against any country or any aspirations on the Earth, but because the placing of such aspirations in the foreground shows at the very outset that the most intensely personal element is insinuating itself into the true ideal of theosophy.

Many times I have spoken earnest words of the tasks and aims of theosophy. The occultist does not speak without reflection. He knows very well when he must use such words! What I have said to you is entirely remote from any emotion, any desire, any sympathy or antipathy; it is demanded by something you may perhaps yourselves realize—namely, the seriousness of the hour—I mean, for theosophy, for occultism. As I have so often said, theosophy must draw from the well-springs of human wisdom the message that is needful for mankind in the present age. If theosophy is to move towards this ideal, it must stand on its own feet, set up its own rules of conduct—not only for what it has to say, but for how it has to confront the world—in order that standards prevailing in the outside world shall not play into our theosophical movement. For there they become an evil, a great evil. As often as certain usages current in the outside world are introduced into the theosophical movement, just so often is the theosophical handed over to the forces of destruction. To outside eyes, these usages, when introduced into theosophy, sometimes assume so grotesque a form that the world will certainly take good care not to copy things that may grow from the rich and fertile soil of occultism. Every kind of league exists in the world today—for the promotion of peace, vegetarianism, anti-alcoholism, and what not—all of which are perfectly justifiable goals. But when the basic principles of a society are stretched in order to include the foundation of unions or even orders connected with the coming of figureheads, founders of religion—unions or orders for the coming of future World Saviors[†]—then the outside world will certainly not follow suit! I cannot imagine that a statesman would found a league to await the coming of a new statesman, or a general to await the coming of a great general in the future!

These things are so simple that only a little reflection is necessary. For to found an Order to await the coming of a World Savior is just as grotesque as it would be to found a league to await the coming of a new statesman or a great general. A certain person who is striving today to found a branch of such an order used the following argument to me: "Yes, but after all, in the year 1848 a league was founded for the purpose of uniting the German States—and then there was Bismarck too; he certainly helped to bring the German Reich to birth." I could only reply: "Really? I am not aware that a league was ever founded to await the coming of a Bismarck!"

Do you think I am saying this jokingly? I say it because occultism has also this side to it, that if it is not cultivated in the right way, it can actually undermine instead of develop the powers of judgment, and I say it because I am in deep earnest about these things. Many occult teachings have been gathered together here; in fifty years, possibly, one point or another may have been investigated still more closely, may have to be differently expressed.

But even if no fragment remains of the knowledge that has been brought forward, I do desire that one thing shall have survived—namely, this: that here there was inaugurated and sustained a theosophical-occult movement taking its stand solely and entirely upon integrity and truth. Even if in fifty years it is already said, "Everything must be corrected; but at least they were out to be true, to let nothing happen except what is true," even then my ideal would have been attained. That integrity and truth can prevail in an occult movement, whatever storms may rise up against us in the world—I am not so arrogant as to say that this has been "achieved," but rather that this is the goal towards which we have striven.

EDITORIAL AND REFERENCE NOTES

On this edition

These lectures were given to members of the Besant Branch, founded and led by Rudolf Steiner and Marie Steiner-von Sivers in Berlin (renamed the "Berlin Branch" after the separation from the Theosophical Society). They were not a self-contained lecture cycle but part of the ongoing work of the branch.

Textual basis: The German edition follows the text version prepared by Walther Vegelahn on the basis of his shorthand notes.

The *title of the volume* goes back to the first reproduction of 1917 as a manuscript print for the members with the designation "Cycle 36" and the title *Der irdische und der kosmische Mensch* [Earthly and cosmic man].

Paul Gerhard Bellmann was responsible for reviewing the 4th German edition of 1989. The notes were improved and supplemented.

At the time when Rudolf Steiner gave these lectures, he still stood within the Theosophical Society with his anthroposophically oriented spiritual science and used the words "theosophy" and "theosophical," but always in the sense of his spiritual science, which was anthroposophically oriented from the beginning. In accordance with a later statement by Rudolf Steiner, these terms are generally replaced here by "spiritual science" or "anthroposophy," "spiritual-scientific" or "anthroposophical."

Notes on the text

Works by Rudolf Steiner within the Collected Works (CW) are indicated in the notes with the bibliographic number. See also the overview at the end of the volume.

1 **the meeting at Munich**
The Portal of Initiation and, as a world premiere, *The Soul's Probation* by Rudolf Steiner were performed; before that, *The Sacred Drama of Eleusis* by Edouard Schuré, translated by Marie Steiner-von Sivers and reworked by Rudolf Steiner.

2 ***The Soul's Probation***
See Rudolf Steiner, *Four Mystery Dramas* (CW 14).

3 **Architektenhaus**
In the former Berlin Architektenhaus at Wilhelmstraße 92/93. Rudolf Steiner gave most of his public lectures in Berlin there in the period 1902–1918.

a building in Munich
The building first planned for Munich was later built as the Goetheanum in Dornach, Switzerland.

3 **the first house for anthroposophy existing in Central Europe**
See the Stuttgart lectures of October 15 and 16, 1911, on the esoteric significance of the Stuttgart building, in *Rosicrucianism Renewed* (CW 284).

4 **lectures . . . in Lugano, Locarno, Milan, Neuchâtel and Berne**
See Rudolf Steiner, *Esoteric Christianity and the Mission of Christian Rosenkreutz* (CW 130).

5 **Mystery of the Resurrection**
See Rudolf Steiner, *From Jesus to Christ* (CW 131).

words of St. Paul
1 Cor. 15:14

6 **H. P. Blavatsky**
Helena Petrovna Blavatsky (1831–1891). Daughter of Colonel Peter von Hahn, granddaughter of Lieutenant-General Alexis von Rottenstein-Hahn, of the Mecklenburg family in Ekaterinoslav, Russia. Gifted with strong psychic powers during childhood, but also very self-willed. At 18, in rebellion against her family, she married the Vice-Governor of Eriwan (Caucasus) Nikofor von Blavatsky (thirty years older than she), whom she divorced almost immediately. In the following years, she began long journeys across various continents. In August 1851 in London, she met her spiritual leader, "Mahatma M" of theosophical literature, whom she had known in visions since childhood. He instructed her to prepare herself through study and occult training for work within an occult society. In 1873 she travelled to New York on his inner directions to oppose and clarify the spiritualism then rampant in America. This led her to connect with Colonel Olcott, and in the autumn of 1875, the Theosophical Society was founded, the headquarters of which was moved to India in 1879. Whereas Olcott organized and administered the Society, H. P. B. was its spiritual center. She wrote her great works *Isis Unveiled* (1877), *The Secret Doctrine* (1888), *The Key to Theosophy* (1889), *The Voice of the Silence* (1889). She left India in 1886 and thereafter lived (between short stays in Würzburg and Ostende) in London. [Note by Paul Marshall Allen.]

7 **an oriental form of theosophy**
See Rudolf Steiner, *Autobiography* (CW 28), chap. 65.

9 **Annie Besant**
Annie Besant (b. Wood, in London, 1847, d. 1933 in Adyar, India), of Irish ancestry, religiously brought up, married Anglican Minister Frank Besant in 1867, and separated in 1873. A period of important activity as a free-thinker and a socialist followed. At the time, she was acclaimed the best public speaker in England, and an expert on hypnotism and spiritualism; when *The Secret Doctrine* by Blavatsky appeared in 1888, she was asked to review it. Greatly impressed, she managed to meet Blavatsky, became her personal pupil, joined the Theosophical Society, and deserted her former companions. After that, she devoted herself entirely to theosophy and, through Blavatsky, came into contact with the Masters. After Blavatsky's death, she succeeded Blavatsky as the leader of the Esoteric School, and

after the death of the Founder-President, Olcott, she became the President of the Theosophical Society. She also played a part in public affairs in India. Under her presidency, the Central Hindu College in Benares was founded in 1889, from which the Hindu University developed. During the First World War, she was interned by the Anglo-Indian government because she supported the Indians in their struggle for home rule. For a time, she was also the president of the Indian National Congress until 1920, when she retired from active politics. Whereas she acquired great merit up to her election as President of the Theosophical Society in 1907, after that time, she branched off more and more in the direction of an authoritative personal cult. That led to great difficulties in the Society and many of the oldest and best members left or withdrew. The questionable manner of her leadership of the Society and her propagation of the Order of the Star of the East, led to a break with Rudolf Steiner. See *Annie Besant: An Autobiography* (Pasadena, CA, 1983); Anne Taylor, *Annie Besant: A Biography* (Oxford, 1992); Arthur H. Nethercot, *The First Five Lives of Annie Besant* (London, 1961); Bhagavan Das, *The Central Hindu College and Mrs. Besant* (Berlin, 1914). On the split in the Society and the exclusion of the German Section from the Theosophical Society, see Eugen Levy, *Mrs. Besant and the Crisis in the Theosophical Society*; and Carl Unger, *Wider literarisches Freibeutertum! Eine Abfertigung des Herrn Dr. Hübbe-Schleiden* [Against Literary Free booting! A Reproof of Dr. Hübbe-Schleiden] (Berlin, 1913). [Note by Paul Marshall Allen.]

11 ***The Spiritual Guidance of the Individual and Humanity***
Rudolf Steiner, *The Spiritual Guidance of the Individual and Humanity* (CW 15).

the greatest teacher of Christianity
See Rudolf Steiner, *Esoteric Christianity and the Mission of Christian Rosenkreutz* (CW 130).

12 ***The Changing World***
Annie Besant, *The Changing World and Lectures to Theosophical Students: Fifteen Lectures delivered in London during May, June, and July 1909* (London: The Theosophical Publishing Society, 1910).

the Mexican deities Quetzalcoatl and Tezcatlipoca
See Rudolf Steiner, *Inner Impulses of Evolution: The Mexican Mysteries and the Knights Templar* (CW 171).

13 **speaking about Christian Rosenkreutz here**
See Rudolf Steiner, *Inner Experiences of Evolution* (CW 132).

19 **in one of the last public lectures**
See the lecture of January 4, 1912, in *Menschengeschichte im Lichte der Geistesforschung* [Human history in the light of spiritual research] (CW 61).

22 **remnants of Atlantean races**
"Races," according to Steiner, did not exist in the early period of human evolution on Earth; they arose in a certain period and will dissolve again in the future. In Steiner's view, one has to be clear "that the concept of race

ceases to have any meaning especially in our time" (lecture of December 4, 1909, in *The Universal Human* [CW 117]). Rudolf Steiner's published work consists of a variety of written texts produced over a span of decades, as well as transcripts of lectures given to various audiences—both invitation-only and public—which have not been reviewed or corrected by the author. The core concern of Steiner's philosophy and anthroposophy, in theory and practice, is the emancipatory development of the free, self-determined individual on a path of knowledge, irrespective of any ethnic or other characteristics. Rudolf Steiner advocated the principle of brotherhood in society. Taken as a whole, his work does not contain any teaching from which racism could be derived. However, like any work, it is not immune to misuse, whether by followers or opponents. Nowhere in his writings or lectures did Steiner call for hatred or discrimination against specific groups. On the contrary, he repeatedly took a strong stand against racial, ethnic, nationalistic, and gender discrimination. This should be kept in mind when reading statements about cultures, "races," and peoples.

23 **Martin Buber**
Martin Buber, (1878–1965), Austrian-Israeli philosopher. See *Chinesische Geister- und Liebesgeschichten* [Chinese ghost and love stories] (Frankfurt a. M., 1911).

24 **the light shed upon the wisdom of India by Friedrich Schlegel**
Friedrich Schlegel (1772–1829), German poet, philosopher, Indologist. See *Von der Sprache und Weisheit der Inder* [On the language and wisdom of the Indians] (1808).

Schopenhauer
Arthur Schopenhauer (1788–1860), German philosopher. See *Sämtliche Werke in 12 Bdn. mit Einleitung von Dr. Rudolf Steiner* [Collected works in 12 volumes, with an introduction by Dr. Rudolf Steiner] (Stuttgart and Berlin o.J.,1894–96).

Eduard von Hartmann
Eduard von Hartmann (1842–1906), German philosopher. Von Hartmann became an officer in the Prussian army. Because of an illness, he retired from military service and began an intensive study of philosophy. The appearance of his *Philosophy of the Unconscious* in 1869 brought him instant fame. He wrote many philosophical books and essays and died in 1906.

25 **our friend Michael Bauer**
Michael Bauer (1871–1929), German teacher, author, and anthroposophist.

34 **Friedrich Theodor Vischer**
Friedrich Theodor Vischer (1807–1887), German novelist, poet, playwright, and art historian.

39 **the saying of Goethe**
From *Faust I*, Auerbachs Cellar.

"The Relation of the I to Thinking"
Richard Eriksen, "Jeget og Taenkningen" [The I and thinking].

The Philosophy of Freedom
Rudolf Steiner, *The Philosophy of Freedom: The Basis for a Modern World Conception, Results of Soul Observation According to the Natural-scientific Method* (CW 4).

Truth and Science
Rudolf Steiner, *Truth and Science* (CW 3).

40 an old German professor
Presumably Adolf Lasson, Berlin. See the following newspaper article.

excerpt from the *Frankfurter Zeitung*
Frankfurter Zeitung, no. 174, December 15, 1912.

41 in the first chapter of the Gospel of Mark
Mark 1:15.

43 the anthroposophical calendar which has just been published
Rudolf Steiner, *The Calendar of the Soul* (in CW 40).

Fräulein von Eckhardtstein
Imme von Eckhardtstein (1871–1930).

45 *Kalevala*
A collection of Finnish legends transmitted orally until published in the nineteenth century, and now regarded as the Finnish national epic.

48 the public lectures given in the Berlin Architektenhaus
See *Menschengeschichte im Lichte der Geistesforschung* [Human history in the light of spiritual research] (CW 61).

51 the public lecture which I was able to give
See Rudolf Steiner, *Our Connection with the Elemental World: Kalevala – Olaf Åsteson – the Russian People: The World as the Result of Balancing Influences* (CW 158).

52 *The Portal of Initiation*
See Rudolf Steiner, *Four Mystery Dramas* (CW 14).

53 *The Education of the Child in the Light of Spiritual Science*
This essay was translated and published in English as a booklet already in 1909, having been published in German in 1907. It went through many subsequent editions and is currently available in *The Education of the Child and Early Lectures on Education* (SteinerBooks, 1996).

60 a king in the realm of the Shades
Homer's *Odyssey*, Canto 11 verses 489–491, words of Achilles.

62 "The Prophet Elijah in the Light of Spiritual Science"
In Rudolf Steiner, *Menschengeschichte im Lichte der Geistesforschung* [Human history in the light of spiritual research] (CW 61).

65 Bernini
Lorenzo Bernini (1598–1680), Italian architect, sculptor, and painter.

Voltaire's works
Voltaire (born Francois-Marie Arouet; 1694–1778), French Enlightenment writer, philosopher, satirist, and historian.

68 Novalis
Novalis (born Friedrich Leopold Freiherr von Hardenberg; 1772–1801), German poet, novelist, and philosopher.

69 Herman Grimm
Herman Grimm (1828–190), German writer and art historian. See *The Life of Raphael* (Boston: Cupples and Hurd, 1888).

71 Anastasius Grün
Anastasius Grün (born Count Anton Alexander von Auersperg; 1806–1876).

73 for roses there
From "Fünf Ostern" [Five Easters] in the collection of poems *Schutt* [Debris] (1835), trans. C. F. B. and C. V.

82 Nietzsche
Friedrich Nietzsche (1844–1900), German philosopher.

89 the lectures on the Apocalypse
Rudolf Steiner, *The Apocalypse of St John* (CW 104).

100 Giovanni Santi
Giovanni Santi (c. 1440–1494), Italian painter and decorator; father of Raphael.

103 *Occult Science*
Rudolf Steiner, *An Outline of Occult Science* (CW 13).

118 *The Spiritual Guidance of the Individual and Humanity*
Rudolf Steiner, *The Spiritual Guidance of the Individual and Humanity* (CW 15).

121 *Christianity as Mystical Fact*
Rudolf Steiner, *Christianity as a Mystical Fact and the Mysteries of Antiquity* (CW 8).

122 "Man in the Light of Occultism, Theosophy and Philosophy"
Rudolf Steiner, *Man in the Light of Occultism, Theosophy and Philosophy* (CW 137).

124 H. P. Blavatsky
See note to page 6.

126 Walther Rathenau
Walther Rathenau (1867–1922), member of the German government after the First World War, was shot by nationalists in May 1922. *Zur Kritik der Zeit* [Toward a critique of the age] (Berlin, 1911).

129 unions or orders for the coming of future World Saviors
Note added by Rudolf Steiner to this passage in the 1917 edition: "For those who have only recently become acquainted with the anthroposophical worldview, it should be noted here that the above words were spoken at the time when Mrs. Besant had founded the Order of the Star of the East with aims such as those indicated above, which I rejected. Incidentally, Mrs. Besant's later hateful agitation against German culture is a genuine fruit of her aberrations, which were already apparent at that time."

RUDOLF STEINER'S COLLECTED WORKS

The German Edition of Rudolf Steiner's Collected Works (the *Gesamtausgabe* [GA], published by Rudolf Steiner Verlag, Dornach, Switzerland) will be completed in the year 2025. The works are organized either by type of work (written, spoken, artistic creations), chronology, audience (public or other), or subject (education, art, etc.). For ease of comparison, the Collected Works in English (CW), listed below, follows the German organization and numbering.

The volumes that have so far been published in the English Collected Works edition appear *in italics with their published titles*; all other volumes, including those that have appeared in editions other than the CW, are set in Roman type with *literal translations* of the German titles. Published English titles are not necessarily the same as the German.

This list is current as of the date of this volume's publication.

A. Written Works

I. Writings 1884–1925

CW 1	Introductions and Selected Commentary on Goethe's Natural-scientific Writings
CW 1a–e	Goethe's Natural-scientific Writings
CW 1f	Editorial Afterwords to Goethe's Natural-scientific Writings in the Weimar Edition (1891–1896)
CW 2	*Goethe's Theory of Knowledge: An Outline of the Epistemology of His Worldview*
CW 3	Truth and Science
CW 4	The Philosophy of Freedom
CW 4a	Documents to "The Philosophy of Freedom"
CW 5	Friedrich Nietzsche, A Fighter against His Own Time
CW 6	Goethe's Worldview
CW 7	Mysticism at the Dawn of Modern Spiritual Life and Its Relationship with Modern Worldviews
CW 8	*Christianity as Mystical Fact and the Mysteries of Antiquity*
CW 9	Theosophy: An Introduction into Supersensible World Knowledge and Human Purpose
CW 10	How Does One Attain Knowledge of Higher Worlds?
CW 11	From the Akasha-Chronicle
CW 12	Levels of Higher Knowledge
CW 13	Occult Science in Outline
CW 14	*Four Modern Mystery Dramas*
CW 15	The Spiritual Guidance of the Individual and Humanity
CW 16/17	*A Way of Self-Knowledge & The Threshold of the Spiritual World*

CW 18 The Riddles of Philosophy in Their History, Presented as an Outline
CW 18a Views of the World and of Life in the Nineteenth Century
CW 19 Thoughts during the Time of War (1915) and Further Texts on the Events of the World War (1917–1921)
CW 20 The Riddles of the Human Being: Articulated and Unarticulated in the Thinking, Views and Opinions of a Series of German and Austrian Personalities
CW 21 The Riddles of the Soul
CW 22 Goethe's Spiritual Nature and Its Revelation in "Faust" and through the "Fairy Tale of the Snake and the Lily"
CW 23 The Central Points of the Social Question in the Necessities of Life in the Present and the Future
CW 24 Essays Concerning the Threefold Division of the Social Organism and the Period 1915–1921
CW 25 Three Steps of Anthroposophy. Philosophy – Cosmology – Religion
CW 26 Anthroposophical Leading Thoughts
CW 27 Fundamentals for Expansion of the Art of Healing according to Spiritual-Scientific Insights
CW 28 *Autobiography: Chapters in the Course of My Life: 1861–1907*

II. Collected Essays

CW 29 Collected Essays on Dramaturgy, 1889–1900
CW 30 Methodical Foundations of Anthroposophy: Collected Essays on Philosophy, Natural Science, Aesthetics and Psychology, 1884–1901
CW 31 Collected Essays on Culture and Current Events, 1887–1901
CW 32 Collected Essays on Literature, 1884–1902
CW 33 Biographies and Biographical Sketches, 1894–1905
CW 34 Lucifer-Gnosis: Foundational Essays on Anthroposophy and Reports from the Periodicals "Luzifer" and "Lucifer-Gnosis," 1903–1908
CW 35 Philosophy and Anthroposophy: Collected Essays, 1904–1923
CW 36 The Goetheanum-Idea in the Middle of the Cultural Crisis of the Present: Collected Essays from the Periodical "Das Goetheanum," 1921–1925
CW 37 Writings on the History of the Anthroposophical Movement and Society 1902–1925

III. Publications from the Literary Estate

CW 38/1 Complete Letters, Vol. 1: Weimar Period 1879–1890
CW 38/2 Complete Letters, Vol. 2: Weimar Period 1890–1897

CW 38/3 Complete Letters, Vol. 3: Early Berlin Period 1897–1905 [forthcoming]
CW 38/4 Complete Letters, Vol. 4: Activity within the Theosophical Society 1905–1912 [forthcoming]
CW 38/5 Complete Letters, Vol. 5: From the Founding of the Anthroposophical Society to the Opening of the Goetheanum 1913–1920 [forthcoming]
CW 38/6 Complete Letters, Vol. 6: The Last Years 1920–1925 [forthcoming]
CW 40 Truth-Wrought Words
CW 40a Sayings, Poems and Mantras; Supplementary Volume
CW 41a Translations and Free Renderings from the Old and New Testaments
CW 41b Translations and Free Renderings of Various Works
CW 42 Stage Adaptations I: Dramas by Edouard Schuré
CW 43 Stage Adaptations II: The Oberufer Christmas Plays
CW 44 Sketches, Fragments and Paralipomena on the Four Mystery Dramas
CW 45 Anthroposophy: A Fragment from the Year 1910
CW 46 Posthumous Essays and Fragments 1879–1924
CW 47/48 Notebooks and Notepads (digital edition)
CW 49 Notes for and about Helmuth and Eliza von Moltke and Relatives, 1904–1924 [forthcoming]
CW 50 [Blank number]

B. Lectures

I. Public Lectures

CW 51 *On Philosophy, History, and Literature: Lectures at the Worker Education School and the Independent College, Berlin, 1901–1905*
CW 52 Spiritual Teachings Concerning the Soul and Observation of the World
CW 53 The Origin and Goal of the Human Being
CW 54 The Riddles of the World and Anthroposophy
CW 55 Knowledge of the Supersensible in Our Times and Its Meaning for Life Today
CW 56 Knowledge of the Soul and of the Spirit
CW 57 Where and How Does One Find the Spirit?
CW 58 The Metamorphoses of the Soul Life. Paths of Soul Experiences: Part One
CW 59 The Metamorphoses of the Soul Life. Paths of Soul Experiences: Part Two
CW 60 The Answers of Spiritual Science to the Biggest Questions of Existence
CW 61 Human History in the Light of Spiritual Research

CW 62 *Results of Spiritual Research*
CW 63 Spiritual Science as a Treasure for Life
CW 64 Out of Destiny-Burdened Times
CW 65 Out of Central European Spiritual Life
CW 66 Spirit and Matter, Life and Death
CW 67 The Eternal in the Human Soul. Immortality and Freedom
CW 68a On the Being of Christianity
CW 68b The Cycle of the Human Being within the Sense-, Soul-, and Spirit-World
CW 68c Goethe and the Present
CW 68d The Being of Man in the Light of Spiritual Science
CW 69a Truths and Errors of Spiritual Research. Spiritual Science and the Future of Mankind
CW 69b Knowledge and Immortality
CW 69c New Christ-Experience
CW 69d Death and Immortality in the Light of Spiritual Science
CW 69e Spiritual Science and the Spiritual Goals of Our Time
CW 70a Human Soul, Destiny and Death
CW 70b Paths to the Knowledge of the Eternal Powers of the Human Soul
CW 71a Soul Immortality [forthcoming]
CW 71b The Human Being as a Soul and Spirit Being
CW 72 Freedom – Immortality – Social Life
CW 73 The Supplementing of the Modern Sciences through Anthroposophy
CW 73a Specialized Fields of Knowledge and Anthroposophy
CW 74 The Philosophy of Thomas Aquinas
CW 75 *Anthroposophy and the Natural Sciences: Foundations and Methods*
CW 76 The Fructifying Effect of Anthroposophy on Specialized Fields
CW 77a The Task of Anthroposophy in Relation to Science and Life: The Darmstadt College Course
CW 77b Art and Anthroposophy. The Goetheanum-Impulse
CW 78 Anthroposophy, Its Roots of Knowledge and Fruits for Life
CW 79 The Reality of the Higher Worlds
CW 80a The Being of Anthroposophy
CW 80b The Inner Realm of Nature and the Being of the Human Soul
CW 80c Anthroposophical Spiritual Science and the Great Civilizational Questions of the Present
CW 81 *Reimagining Academic Studies: Science, Philosophy, Education, Social Science, Theology, Theory of Language*
CW 82 *Becoming Fully Human: The Significance of Anthroposophy in Contemporary Spiritual Life*
CW 83 *The Tension between East and West*
CW 84 *The Aims of Anthroposophy and the Purpose of the Goetheanum*

CW 85 Supplementary Volume: Individual Public Lectures I [forthcoming]
CW 86 Supplementary Volume: Individual Public Lectures II [forthcoming]

II. Lectures to the Members of the Anthroposophical Society

CW 87 Ancient Mysteries and Christianity
CW 88 *Concerning the Astral World and Devachan*
CW 89 Consciousness – Life – Form. Fundamental Principles of a Spiritual-Scientific Cosmology
CW 90a Self-knowledge and Knowledge of the Divine, Vol. I. Theosophy, Christology, and Mythology
CW 90b Self-knowledge and Knowledge of the Divine, Vol. II. Theosophy, Christology, and Mythology
CW 90c Theosophy and Occultism
CW 91 Cosmology and Human Evolution. Introduction to Theosophy – Theory of Colors
CW 92 *The Occult Truths of Myths and Legends: Greek and Germanic Mythology: Richard Wagner in the Light of Spiritual Science*
CW 93 The Temple Legend and the Golden Legend as a Symbolic Expression of Past and Future Secrets of Human Development. From the Contents of the Esoteric School
CW 93a Fundamentals of Esotericism
CW 94 Cosmogony. Popular Occultism. The Gospel of John. Theosophy Based on the Gospel of John
CW 95 At the Gates of Theosophy
CW 96 Origin-Impulses of Spiritual Science. Christian Esotericism in the Light of New Spirit-knowledge
CW 97 The Christian Mystery
CW 98 *Nature Beings and Spirit Beings: Their Activity in Our Visible World*
CW 99 The Theosophy of the Rosicrucians
CW 100 *True Knowledge of the Christ: Theosophy and Rosicucianism—The Gospel of John*
CW 101 Myths and Legends. Occult Signs and Symbols
CW 102 *Good and Evil Spirits and Their Influence on Humanity*
CW 103 *The Gospel of John*
CW 104 The Apocalypse of John
CW 104a From the Picture-Script of the Apocalypse of John
CW 105 *Universe, Earth, Human Being: Their Relationship to Egyptian Myths and Modern Civilization*
CW 106 Egyptian Myths and Mysteries in Relation to the Active Spiritual Forces of the Present
CW 107 *Disease, Karma, and Healing: Spiritual-scientific Enquiries into the Nature of the Human Being*

CW 108 Answering the Questions of Life and the World through Anthroposophy
CW 109 The Principle of Spiritual Economy in Connection with the Question of Reincarnation. An Aspect of the Spiritual Guidance of Humanity
CW 110 *The Spiritual Hierarchies and the Physical World: Zodiac, Planets, and Cosmos*
CW 111 Introduction to the Foundations of Theosophy
CW 112 The Gospel of John in Relation to the Three Other Gospels, Especially the Gospel of Luke
CW 113 The Orient in the Light of the Occident. The Children of Lucifer and the Brothers of Christ
CW 114 The Gospel of Luke
CW 115 Anthroposophy – Psychosophy – Pneumatosophy
CW 116 *The Christ-Impulse and the Development of Ego-Consciousness*
CW 117 *Deeper Secrets of Human Evolution in Light of the Gospels*
CW 117a The Gospel of John and the Three Other Gospels
CW 118 The Event of the Christ-Appearance in the Etheric World
CW 119 *Macrocosm and Microcosm: The Greater and the Lesser World: Questions Concerning the Soul, Life and the Spirit*
CW 120 The Revelations of Karma
CW 121 *The Mission of Folk Souls*
CW 122 The Secrets of the Biblical Creation-Story. The Six-Day Work in the First Book of Moses
CW 123 The Gospel of Matthew
CW 124 *Background to the Gospel of St. Mark*
CW 125 *Paths and Goals of the Spiritual Human Being: Life Questions in the Light of Spiritual Science*
CW 126 Occult History. Esoteric Observations of the Karmic Relationships of Personalities and Events of World History
CW 127 *The Mission of the New Spiritual Revelation: The Pivotal Nature of the Christ Event in Earth Evolution*
CW 128 An Occult Physiology
CW 129 *Wonders of the World: Trials of the Soul, Revelations of the Spirit*
CW 130 Esoteric Christianity and the Spiritual Guidance of Humanity
CW 131 *From Jesus to Christ*
CW 132 *Inner Experiences of Evolution*
CW 133 *Earthly and Cosmic Man*
CW 134 *The World of the Senses and the World of the Spirit*
CW 135 Reincarnation and Karma and Their Meaning for the Culture of the Present
CW 136 *Spiritual Beings in the Heavenly Bodies and in the Kingdoms of Nature*

CW 137 The Human Being in the Light of Occultism, Theosophy and Philosophy
CW 138 On Initiation. On Eternity and the Passing Moment. On the Light of the Spirit and the Darkness of Life
CW 139 The Gospel of Mark
CW 140 Occult Investigation into the Life between Death and New Birth. The Living Interaction between Life and Death
CW 141 *Between Death and Rebirth: In Relation to Cosmic Facts*
CW 142/46 *The Bhagavad Gita and the West: The Esoteric Significance of the Bhagavad Gita and Its Relation to the Epistles of Paul*
CW 143 *Three Paths to Christ: Experiencing the Supersensible*
CW 144 *The Mysteries of Initiation: From Isis to the Holy Grail*
CW 145 What Significance Does Occult Development of the Human Being Have for the Sheaths – Physical Body, Etheric Body, Astral Body, and Self?
CW 146 [See CW 142/46]
CW 147 The Secrets of the Threshold
CW 148 The Fifth Gospel
CW 149 *Christ and the Spiritual World: The Quest for the Holy Grail*
CW 150 *How the Spiritual World Projects into Physical Existence: The Influence of the Dead*
CW 151 *Human and Cosmic Thought*
CW 152 *Approaching the Mystery of Golgotha*
CW 153 The Inner Being of Man and Life Between Death and New Birth
CW 154 How Does One Gain an Understanding of the Spiritual World? The Flowing in of Spiritual Impulses from out of the World of the Deceased
CW 155 *Christ and the Human Soul: The Meaning of Life – The Spiritual Foundation of Morality – Anthroposophy and Christianity*
CW 156 *Inner Reading and Inner Hearing: And How to Achieve Existence in the World of Ideas*
CW 157 Human Destinies and the Destiny of Peoples
CW 157a The Formation of Destiny and the Life after Death
CW 158 *Our Connection with the Elemental World: Kalevala – Olaf Åsteson – the Russian People: The World as the Result of Balancing Influences*
CW 159 *The Mystery of Death: The Nature and Significance of Central Europe and the European Folk-Spirits*
CW 160 [Blank number]
CW 161 *Artistic Sensitivity as a Spiritual Approach to Knowing Life and the World*
CW 162 Questions of Art and Life in Light of Spiritual Science
CW 163 Coincidence, Necessity and Providence. Imaginative Knowledge and the Processes after Death

CW 164 *The Value of Thinking for a Cognition that Satisfies the Human Being: The Relationship between Spiritual Science and Natural Science*
CW 165 *Unifying Humanity Spiritually through the Christ Impulse*
CW 166 *Necessity and Freedom*
CW 167 *The Human Spirit Past and Present: Occult Fraternities and the Mystery of Golgotha*
CW 168 *The Connection between the Living and the Dead*
CW 169 World-being and Selfhood
CW 170 The Riddle of the Human Being. The Spiritual Background of Human History
CW 171 Inner Development-Impulses of Humanity. Goethe and the Crisis of the 19th Century.
CW 172 The Karma of the Vocation of the Human Being in Connection with Goethe's Life.
CW 173a Observations of Modern History, Vol. I: Paths to an Objective Judgment
CW 173b Observations of Modern History, Vol. II: The Karma of Untruthfulness
CW 173c Observations of Modern History, Vol. III: The Reality of Occult Impulses
CW 174a *Europe Between East and West in Cosmic and Human History*
CW 174b *The Spiritual Background to the First World War*
CW 175 *Building Stones for an Understanding of the Mystery of Golgotha: Human Life in a Cosmic Context*
CW 176 *The Karma of Materialism: Aspects of Human Evolution*
CW 177 *The Fall of the Spirits of Darkness: The Spiritual Background to the Outer World: Spiritual Beings and Their Effects*
CW 178 Individual Spiritual Beings and Their Influence in the Soul of the Human Being
CW 179 *The Influence of the Dead on Destiny*
CW 180 Mystery Truths and Christmas Impulses. Ancient Myths and their Meaning.
CW 181 *Dying Earth and Living Cosmos: The Living Gifts of Anthroposophy: The Need for New Forms of Consciousness*
CW 182 Death as Transformation of Life
CW 183 *Human Evolution: A Spiritual-Scientific Quest*
CW 184 *Eternal and Transient Elements in Human Life: The Cosmic Past of Humanity and the Mystery of Evil*
CW 185 Historical Symptomology
CW 185a Historical-Developmental Foundations for Forming a Social Judgment
CW 186 The Fundamental Social Demands of Our Time. In Changed Times

CW 187 How Can Humanity Find the Christ Again? The Threefold Shadow-Existence of our Time and the New Christ-Light
CW 188 *Goetheanism: An Impulse of Transformation and Resurrection*
CW 189 *Conscious Society: Anthroposophy and the Social Question*
CW 190 *Past and Future Impulses in Societal Events*
CW 191 *Understanding Society through Spiritual-Scientific Knowledge: Social Threefolding, Christ, Lucifer, and Ahriman*
CW 192 Spiritual-Scientific Treatment of Social and Pedagogical Questions
CW 193 *Problems of Society: An Esoteric View, from Luciferic Past to Ahrimanic Future*
CW 194 *Michael's Mission: Revealing the Essential Secrets of Human Nature*
CW 195 *Cosmic New Year: Thoughts for New Year 1920*
CW 196 *What Is Necessary in These Urgent Times*
CW 197 *Polarities in the Evolution of Humanity: West and East – Materialism and Mysticism – Knowledge and Belief*
CW 198 *Healing the Social Organism*
CW 199 Spiritual Science as Knowledge of the Foundational Impulses of Social Formation
CW 200 The New Spirituality and the Christ-Experience of the 20th Century
CW 201 The Correspondences Between Microcosm and Macrocosm. The Human Being – A Hieroglyph of the Universe.
CW 202 *Universal Spirituality and Human Physicality: Bridging the Divide: The Search for the New Isis and the Divine Sophia*
CW 203 The Responsibility of Human Beings for the Development of the World through their Spiritual Connection with the Planet Earth and the World of the Stars.
CW 204 Perspectives of the Development of Humanity. The Materialistic Knowledge-Impulse and the Task of Anthroposophy.
CW 205 Human Development, World-Soul, and World-Spirit. Part One: The Human Being as a Being of Body and Soul in Relationship to the World.
CW 206 Human Development, World-Soul, and World-Spirit. Part Two: The Human Being as a Spiritual Being in the Process of Historical Development
CW 207 Anthroposophy as Cosmosophy. Part One: Characteristic Features of the Human Being in the Earthly and the Cosmic Realms
CW 208 Anthroposophy as Cosmosophy. Part Two: The Forming of the Human Being as the Result of Cosmic Influence
CW 209 *The Language of the Cosmos: Cosmic Influences and the Spiritual Task of Northern Europe*
CW 210 Old and New Methods of Initiation. Drama and Poetry in the Change of Consciousness in the Modern Age

CW 211 *The Sun Mystery and the Mystery of Death and Resurrection: Exoteric and Esoteric Christianity*
CW 212 *Life of the Human Soul: And Its Relation to World Evolution*
CW 213 *Human Questions and Cosmic Answers*
CW 214 The Mystery of the Trinity: The Human Being in Relationship with the Spiritual World in the Course of Time
CW 215 Philosophy, Cosmology, and Religion in Anthroposophy
CW 216 *Supersensible Impulses in the Historical Development of Humanity*
CW 217 *Becoming the Archangel Michael's Companions: Rudolf Steiner's Challenge to the Younger Generation*
CW 217a *Youth and the Etheric Heart: Rudolf Steiner Speaks to the Younger Generation*
CW 218 *Spirit as Sculptor of the Human Organism*
CW 219 The Relationship of the World of the Stars to the Human Being, and of the Human Being to the World of the Stars. The Spiritual Communion of Humanity
CW 220 *Awake! For the Sake of the Future*
CW 221 Earth-Knowing and Heaven-Insight
CW 222 *The Driving Force of Spiritual Powers in World History*
CW 223 The Cycle of the Year as Breathing Process of the Earth and the Four Great Festival-Seasons. Anthroposophy and the Human Heart (*Gemüt*)
CW 224 The Human Soul and its Connection with Divine-Spiritual Individualities. The Internalization of the Festivals of the Year
CW 225 *Three Perspectives of Anthroposophy: Cultural Phenomena from the Point of View of Spiritual Science*
CW 226 Human Being, Human Destiny, and World Development
CW 227 Initiation-Knowledge
CW 228 *Initiation Science: And the Development of the Human Mind*
CW 229 The Experiencing of the Course of the Year in Four Cosmic Imaginations
CW 230 The Human Being as Harmony of the Creative, Building, and Formative World-Word
CW 231 The Supersensible Human Being, Understood Anthroposophically
CW 232 The Forming of the Mysteries
CW 233 *World History and the Mysteries in the Light of Anthroposophy*
CW 233a *Rosicrucianism and Modern Initiation: Mystery Centres of the Middle Ages: The Easter Festival and the History of the Mysteries*
CW 234 Anthroposophy. A Summary after 21 Years
CW 235 Esoteric Observations of Karmic Relationships in 6 Volumes, Vol. 1
CW 236 Esoteric Observations of Karmic Relationships in 6 Volumes, Vol. 2

CW 237 Esoteric Observations of Karmic Relationships in 6 Volumes, Vol. 3: The Karmic Relationships of the Anthroposophical Movement
CW 238 Esoteric Observations of Karmic Relationships in 6 Volumes, Vol. 4: The Spiritual Life of the Present in Relationship to the Anthroposophical Movement
CW 239 Esoteric Observations of Karmic Relationships in 6 Volumes, Vol. 5
CW 240 Esoteric Observations of Karmic Relationships in 6 Volumes, Vol. 6
CW 241 [Blank number]
CW 242 [Blank number]
CW 243 *True and False Paths of Spiritual Research*
CW 244 Answers to Questions, and Interviews
CW 245 [Blank number]
CW 246 Supplementary Volume I: Individual Members Lectures
CW 247 Supplementary Volume II: Individual Members Lectures
CW 248 [Blank number]
CW 249 [Blank number]
CW 250 On the History of the German Section of the Theosophical Society 1902–1913. Lectures, Speeches, Reports, and Minutes
CW 251 On the History of the Anthroposophical Society 1913–1922
CW 252 On the History of the Building Association and the Goetheanum Association 1911–1924
CW 253 *Sexuality, Inner Development, and Community Life: Ethical and Spiritual Dimensions of the Crisis in the Anthroposophical Society in Dornach, 1915*
CW 254 The Occult Movement in the 19th Century and Its Relationship to World Culture. Significant Points from the Exoteric Cultural Life around the Middle of the 19th Century
CW 255b Anthroposophy and Its Opponents
CW 256 [Blank number]
CW 257 Anthroposophical Community-Building
CW 258 *The Anthroposophic Movement: The History and Conditions of the Anthroposophical Movement in Relation to the Anthroposophical Society: An Encouragement for Self-Examination*
CW 259 The Year of Destiny 1923 in the History of the Anthroposophical Society. From the Burning of the Goetheanum to the Christmas Conference
CW 260 The Christmas Conference for the Founding of the General Anthroposophical Society 1923/24
CW 260a The Constitution of the General Anthroposophical Society and the School for Spiritual Science. The Rebuilding of the Goetheanum
CW 261 *Our Dead: Memorial, Funeral, and Cremation Addresses 1906–1924*

CW 262	Rudolf Steiner and Marie Steiner-von Sivers: Correspondence and Documents, 1901–1925
CW 263/1	Rudolf Steiner and Edith Maryon: Correspondence: Letters, Verses, Sketches, 1912–1924
CW 264	*From the History and Contents of the First Section of the Esoteric School: Letters, Documents, and Lectures: 1904–1914*
CW 265	*Freemasonry and Ritual Work: The Misraim Service*
CW 265a	Teaching and Instruction Lessons for Members of the Knowledge-Cultic Section of the Esoteric School 1904–1914 [forthcoming]
CW 266/1	*From the Esoteric School: Esoteric Lessons 1904–1909*
CW 266/2	*From the Esoteric School: Esoteric Lessons 1910–1912*
CW 266/3	*From the Esoteric School: Esoteric Lessons 1913–1923*
CW 267	*Soul Exercises: Word and Symbol Meditations*
CW 268	*Mantric Sayings: Meditations 1903–1925*
CW 269	Ritual Texts for the Celebration of the Free Christian Religious Instruction. The Collected Verses for Teachers and Students of the Waldorf School
CW 270	Esoteric Instructions for the First Class of the School for Spiritual Science at the Goetheanum 1924, 4 Volumes

III. Lectures and Courses on Specific Realms of Life

Lectures on Art

CW 271	*Art and Theory of Art: Foundations of a New Aesthetics*
CW 272	*Anthroposophy in the Light of Goethe's* Faust*: Volume One of Spiritual-Scientific Commentaries on Goethe's* Faust
CW 273	*Goethe's* Faust *in the Light of Anthroposophy: Volume Two of Spiritual-Scientific Commentaries on Goethe's* Faust
CW 274	Addresses for the Christmas Plays from the Old Folk Traditions
CW 275	Art in the Light of Mystery Wisdom
CW 276	*The Arts and Their Mission*
CW 277a	The Origin and Development of Eurythmy 1912–1918
CW 277b	The Origin and Development of Eurythmy 1918–1920
CW 277c	The Origin and Development of Eurythmy 1920–1922 [forthcoming]
CW 277d	The Origin and Development of Eurythmy 1923–1924 [forthcoming]
CW 278	Eurythmy as Visible Song
CW 279	*Eurythmy as Speech Made Visible: Speech Eurythmy Course*
CW 280	The Method and Nature of Speech Formation
CW 281	The Art of Recitation and Declamation
CW 282	Speech Formation and Dramatic Art
CW 283	*The Inner Nature of Music and the Experience of Tone*
CW 284	*Rosicrucianism Renewed: The Unity of Art, Science & Religion: The Theosophical Congress of Whitsun 1907*

CW 285 [Blank number]
CW 286 Paths to a New Style of Architecture. "And the Building Becomes Man"
CW 287 *Architecture as Peacework: The First Goetheanum, Dornach, 1914*
CW 288 *Architecture, Sculpture, and Painting of the First Goetheanum*
CW 289 The Building-Idea of the Goetheanum: Lectures with Slides from the Years 1920–1921
CW 290 *Toward a New Theory of Architecture: The First Goetheanum in Pictures* [no longer in the German GA]
CW 291 The Being of Colors
CW 291a Knowledge of Colors. Supplementary Volume to "The Being of Colors"
CW 292 *Art History as a Reflection of Inner Spiritual Impulses*

Lectures on Education

CW 293 General Knowledge of the Human Being as the Foundation of Pedagogy
CW 294 The Art of Education: Methodology and Didactics
CW 295 The Art of Education: Seminar Discussions and Lectures on Lesson Planning
CW 296 The Question of Education as a Social Question
CW 297 The Idea and Practice of the Waldorf School
CW 297a Education for Life: Self-Education and the Practice of Pedagogy
CW 298 Rudolf Steiner in the Waldorf School
CW 299 Spiritual-Scientific Observations on Speech
CW 300a Conferences with the Teachers of the Free Waldorf School in Stuttgart, 1919 to 1924, in 3 Volumes, Vol. 1
CW 300b Conferences with the Teachers of the Free Waldorf School in Stuttgart, 1919 to 1924, in 3 Volumes, Vol. 2
CW 300c Conferences with the Teachers of the Free Waldorf School in Stuttgart, 1919 to 1924, in 3 Volumes, Vol. 3
CW 301 The Renewal of Pedagogical-Didactical Art through Spiritual Science
CW 302 Knowledge of the Human Being and the Forming of Class Lessons
CW 302a Education and Teaching from a Knowledge of the Human Being
CW 303 The Healthy Development of the Human Being
CW 304 Methods of Education and Teaching Based on Anthroposophy
CW 304a Anthroposophical Knowledge of the Human Being and Pedagogy
CW 305 The Soul-Spiritual Foundational Forces of the Art of Education. Spiritual Values in Education and Social Life
CW 306 Pedagogical Praxis from the Viewpoint of a Spiritual-Scientific Knowledge of the Human Being. The Education of the Child and Young Human Beings

CW 307 The Spiritual Life of the Present and Education
CW 308 The Method of Teaching and the Life-Requirements for Teaching
CW 309 Anthroposophical Pedagogy and Its Prerequisites
CW 310 The Pedagogical Value of a Knowledge of the Human Being and the Cultural Value of Pedagogy
CW 311 The Art of Education from an Understanding of the Being of Humanity

Lectures on Medicine

CW 312 *Introducing Anthroposophical Medicine*
CW 313 *Illness and Therapy: Spiritual-Scientific Aspects of Healing*
CW 314 *Physiology and Healing: Treatment, Therapy, and Hygiene*
CW 315 Curative Eurythmy
CW 316 *Understanding Healing: Meditative Reflections on Deepening Medicine through Spiritual Science*
CW 317 *Education for Special Needs: The Curative Education Course*
CW 318 The Working Together of Doctors and Pastors
CW 319 *The Healing Process: Spirit, Nature & Our Bodies*

Lectures on Natural Science

CW 320 Spiritual-Scientific Impulses for the Development of Physics 1: The First Natural-Scientific Course: Light, Color, Tone, Mass, Electricity, Magnetism
CW 321 Spiritual-Scientific Impulses for the Development of Physics 2: The Second Natural-Scientific Course: Warmth at the Border of Positive and Negative Materiality
CW 322 The Borders of the Knowledge of Nature
CW 323 *Interdisciplinary Astronomy: Third Scientific Course*
CW 324 Nature Observation, Mathematics, and Scientific Experimentation and Results from the Viewpoint of Anthroposophy
CW 324a The Fourth Dimension in Mathematics and Reality
CW 325 Natural Science and the World-Historical Development of Humanity since Ancient Times
CW 326 The Moment of the Coming Into Being of Natural Science in World History and Its Development Since Then
CW 327 *Agriculture: Spiritual-Scientific Foundations for Agricultural Renewal*

Lectures on Social Life and the Threefold Arrangement of the Social Organism

CW 328 The Social Question
CW 329 The Liberation of the Human Being as the Foundation for a New Social Form

CW 330 The Renewal of the Social Organism
CW 331 Work-Council and Socialization
CW 332a The Social Future
CW 332b Lectures and Speeches on Social and Economic Issues
CW 333 *Freedom of Thought and Societal Forces: Implementing the Demands of Modern Society*
CW 334 From the Unified State to the Threefold Social Organism
CW 335 The Crisis of the Present and the Path to Healthy Thinking
CW 336 The Great Questions of the Times and Anthroposophical Spiritual Knowledge
CW 337a Social Ideas, Social Realities, Social Practice, Vol. 1: Question-and-Answer Evenings and Study Evenings of the Alliance for the Threefold Social Organism in Stuttgart, 1919–1920
CW 337b Social Ideas, Social Realities, Social Practice, Vol. 2: Discussion Evenings of the Swiss Alliance for the Threefold Social Organism
CW 338 *Communicating Anthroposophy: The Course for Speakers to Promote the Idea of Threefolding*
CW 339 Anthroposophy, Threefold Social Organism, and the Art of Public Speaking
CW 340/41 *Rethinking Economics: Lectures and Seminars on World Economics*

Lectures and Courses on Christian Religious Work

CW 342 *First Steps in Christian Religious Renewal: Preparing the Ground for The Christian Community*
CW 343 Lectures and Courses on Christian Religious Work, Vol. 2: Spiritual Knowledge – Religious Feeling – Cultic Doing
CW 344 Lectures and Courses on Christian Religious Work, Vol. 3: Lectures at the Founding of the Christian Community
CW 345 Lectures and Courses on Christian Religious Work, Vol. 4: Concerning the Nature of the Working Word
CW 346 Lectures and Courses on Christian Religious Work, Vol. 5: The Apocalypse and the Work of the Priest

Lectures for Workers at the Goetheanum

CW 347 The Knowledge of the Nature of the Human Being According to Body, Soul and Spirit. On Earlier Conditions of the Earth
CW 348 On Health and Illness. Foundations of a Spiritual-Scientific Doctrine of the Senses
CW 349 On the Life of the Human Being and of the Earth. On the Nature of Christianity
CW 350 Rhythms in the Cosmos and in the Human Being. How Does One Come To See the Spiritual World?

CW 351 The Human Being and the World. The Influence of the Spirit in Nature. On the Nature of Bees

CW 352 Nature and the Human Being Observed Spiritual-Scientifically

CW 353 The History of Humanity and the World-Views of the Folk Cultures

CW 354 The Creation of the World and the Human Being. Life on Earth and the Influence of the Stars

C. Artistic Works

CW A 1–10; 57 The Architectural Work I: The Goetheanum and Its Predecessors

CW A 11 The Sculptural Work

CW A 12 The Goetheanum Windows. The Speech of Light. Sketches and Studies

CW A 13–16; 52–56 The Painting Work

CW A 14 Sketches for the Painting of the Small Dome of the First Goetheanum

CW A 27–43 The Architectural Work II: Commercial and Residential Buildings in Dornach and Other Places [forthcoming]

CW A 45 The Graphic Work

CW A 48 The Drawing Work

CW A 51 The Art of Jewelry as a Goethean Language of Form

CW A 54.0 A Path of Training in Painting. Pastel Sketches and Watercolors

CW A 54.1 Nature Moods. Nine Training Sketches for Painters

Eurythmy Figures

CW A 26 Skectches of the Eurythmy Figures

CW A 26a The Eurythmy Figures of Rudolf Steiner, Artistically Executed by Annemarie Bäschlin

CW A 26b Eurythmy Figures from the Time When They Were Created

Eurythmy Forms

CW A 23/1 Volume I: Eurythmy Forms for Poems by Rudolf Steiner

CW A 23/2 Volume II: Eurythmy Forms for the Calender of the Soul by Rudolf Steiner

CW A 23/3 Volume III: Euythmy Forms for Poems by J. W. von Goethe

CW A 23/4 Volume IV: Eurythmy Forms for Poems by Christian Morgenstern

CW A 23/5 Volume V: Eurythmy Forms for Poems by Albert Steffen

CW A 23/6 Volume VI: Eurythmy Forms for German Poems by Fercher von Steinwand, Hamerling, Hebbel, C. F. Meyer, Nietzsche, among others

CW A 23/7 Volume VII: Eurythmy Forms for English Poems
CW A 23/8 Volume VIII: Eurythmy Forms for French and Russian Poems
CW A 24 Volume IX: Eurythmy Forms for Tone Eurythmy

Blackboard Drawings from Lectures

CW A 58/1 Volume I: 20 Plates from Public Lectures 1920–1924 in CWs 73a, 74, 76, and 84
CW A 58/2 Volume II: 38 Plates from Lectures in 1919 in CWs 191 and 194
CW A 58/3 Volume III: 34 Plates from Lectures in 1920 in CWs 196 and 198
CW A 58/4 Volume IV: 33 Plates from Lectures in 1920 in CWs 199 and 200
CW A 58/5 Volume V: 31 Plates from Lectures in 1920 in CW 201
CW A 58/6 Volume VI: 46 Plates from Lectures 1920–1921 in CWs 202–204
CW A 58/7 Volume VII: 38 Plates from Lectures in 1921 in CWs 205 and 206
CW A 58/8 Volume VIII: 42 Plates from Lectures in 1921 in CWs 207–209
CW A 58/9 Volume IX: 40 Plates from Lectures in 1922 in CWs 210–212
CW A 58/10 Volume X: 35 Plates from Lectures in 1922 in CWs 213–215
CW A 58/11 Volume XI: 41 Plates from Lectures 1922–1923 in CWs 216, 218–220
CW A 58/12 Volume XII: 37 Plates from Lectures in 1923 in CWs 221–225
CW A 58/13 Volume XIII: 38 Plates from Lectures in 1923 in CWs 227–230
CW A 58/14 Volume XIV: 36 Plates from Lectures in 1923 in CWs 232 and 233
CW A 58/15 Volume XV: 37 Plates from Lectures in 1924 in CWs 233a, 234, and 243
CW A 58/16 Volume XVI: 56 Plates from the "Karma Lectures" in CWs 235–238 and 240
CW A 58/17 Volume XVII: 21 Plates from Lectures on the History of the Anthroposophical Society in CWs 257, 258, 260, and 260a
CW A 58/18 Volume XVIII: 33 Plates from Lectures on Art in CWs 271, 276, 283, 288–290, and 291
CW A 58/19 Volume XIX: 41 Plates from Lectures on Eurythmy in CWs 278, 279, and 315
CW A 58/20 Volume XX: 27 Plates from Lectures on Speech Formation in CWs 281 and 282
CW A 58/21 Volume XXI: 42 Plates from Lectures on Education in CWs 296, 303, 304, 306, and 311
CW A 58/22 Volume XXII: 46 Plates from Lectures on Medicine in CWs 312–315
CW A 58/23 Volume XXIII: 48 Plates from Lectures in 1924 in CWs 316–318
CW A 58/24 Volume XXIV: 39 Plates from Lectures on Natural Science and the Social Question in CWs 322, 326, 327, 339, and 340

CW A 58/25 Volume XXV: 33 Plates from the "Workers Lectures" (Volumes 1 and 2) in CWs 347 and 348

CW A 58/26 Volume XXVI: 51 Plates from the "Workers Lectures" (Volumes 3 and 4) in CWs 349 and 350

CW A 58/27 Volume XXVII: 35 Plates from the "Workers Lectures" (Volumes 5 and 6) in CWs 351 and 352

CW A 58/28 Volume XXVIII: 42 Plates from the "Workers Lectures" (Volumes 7 and 8) in CWs 353 and 354

CW A 58/29 Volume XXIX: 43 Plates from Lectures and Courses on Christian Religious Activity in CWs 342–344 and 346

CW A 58/30 Volume XXX: 27 Plates from CWs 255b, 324a, 337b, and 340, Corrigenda, Plates without CW Assignment, Copies

SIGNIFICANT EVENTS IN THE LIFE OF RUDOLF STEINER

1829: June 23: birth of Johann Steiner (1829–1910)—Rudolf Steiner's father—in Geras, Lower Austria.

1834: May 8: birth of Franciska Blie (1834–1918)—Rudolf Steiner's mother—in Horn, Lower Austria. "My father and mother were both children of the glorious Lower Austrian forest district north of the Danube."

1860: May 16: marriage of Johann Steiner and Franciska Blie.

1861: February 25: birth of *Rudolf Joseph Lorenz Steiner* in Kraljevec, Croatia, near the border with Hungary, where Johann Steiner works as a telegrapher for the South Austria Railroad. Rudolf Steiner is baptized two days later, February 27, the date usually given as his birthday.

1862: Summer: the family moves to Mödling, Lower Austria.

1863: The family moves to Pottschach, Lower Austria, near the Styrian border, where Johann Steiner becomes stationmaster. "The view stretched to the mountains...majestic peaks in the distance and the sweet charm of nature in the immediate surroundings."

1864: November 15: birth of Rudolf Steiner's sister, Leopoldine (d. November 1, 1927). She will become a seamstress and live with her parents for the rest of her life.

1866: July 28: birth of Rudolf Steiner's deaf-mute brother, Gustav (d. May 1, 1941).

1867: Rudolf Steiner enters the village school. Following a disagreement between his father and the schoolmaster, whose wife falsely accused the boy of causing a commotion, Rudolf Steiner is taken out of school and taught at home.

1868: A critical experience. Unknown to the family, an aunt dies in a distant town. Sitting in the station waiting room, Rudolf Steiner sees her "form," which speaks to him, asking for help. "Beginning with this experience, a new soul life began in the boy, one in which not only the outer trees and mountains spoke to him, but also the worlds that lay behind them. From this moment on, the boy began to live with the spirits of nature...."

1869: The family moves to the peaceful, rural village of Neudorfl, near Wiener-Neustadt in present-day Austria. Rudolf Steiner attends the village school. Because of the "unorthodoxy" of his writing and spelling, he has to do "extra lessons."

1870: Through a book lent to him by his tutor, he discovers geometry: "To grasp something purely in the spirit brought me inner happiness. I know that I first learned happiness through geometry." The same tutor allows him to draw, while other students still struggle with their reading and writing. "An artistic element" thus enters his education.

1871: Though his parents are not religious, Rudolf Steiner becomes a "church child," a favorite of the priest, who was "an exceptional character." "Up to the age of ten or eleven, among those I came to know, he was far and away the most significant." Among other things, he introduces Steiner to Copernican, heliocentric cosmology. As an altar boy, Rudolf Steiner serves at Masses, funerals, and Corpus Christi processions. At year's end, after an incident in which he escapes a thrashing, his father forbids him to go to church.

1872: Rudolf Steiner transfers to grammar school in Wiener-Neustadt, a five-mile walk from home, which must be done in all weathers.

1873–75: Through his teachers and on his own, Rudolf Steiner has many wonderful experiences with science and mathematics. Outside school, he teaches himself analytic geometry, trigonometry, differential equations, and calculus.

1876: Rudolf Steiner begins tutoring other students. He learns bookbinding from his father. He also teaches himself stenography.

1877: Rudolf Steiner discovers Kant's *Critique of Pure Reason*, which he reads and rereads. He also discovers and reads von Rotteck's *World History*.

1878: He studies extensively in contemporary psychology and philosophy.

1879: Rudolf Steiner graduates from high school with honors. His father is transferred to Inzersdorf, near Vienna. He uses his first visit to Vienna "to purchase a great number of philosophy books"—Kant, Fichte, Schelling, and Hegel, as well as numerous histories of philosophy. His aim: to find a path from the "I" to nature.

October 1879–1883: Rudolf Steiner attends the Technical College in Vienna—to study mathematics, chemistry, physics, mineralogy, botany, zoology, biology, geology, and mechanics—with a scholarship. He also attends lectures in history and literature, while avidly reading philosophy on his own. His two favorite professors are Karl Julius Schröer (German language and literature) and Edmund Reitlinger (physics). He also audits lectures by Robert Zimmerman on aesthetics and Franz Brentano on philosophy. During this year he begins his friendship with Moritz Zitter (1861–1921), who will help support him financially when he is in Berlin.

1880: Rudolf Steiner attends lectures on Schiller and Goethe by Karl Julius Schröer, who becomes his mentor. Also "through a remarkable combination of circumstances," he meets Felix Koguzki, an "herb gatherer" and healer, who could "see deeply into the secrets of nature." Rudolf Steiner will meet and study with this "emissary of the Master" throughout his time in Vienna.

1881: January: "… I didn't sleep a wink. I was busy with philosophical problems until about 12:30 a.m. Then, finally, I threw myself down on my couch. All my striving during the previous year had been to research whether the following statement by Schelling was true or not: *Within everyone dwells a secret, marvelous capacity to draw back from the stream of time—out of the self clothed in all that comes to us from outside—into our innermost being and there, in the immutable form of the Eternal, to look into ourselves.* I believe, and I am still quite certain of it, that I discovered this capacity in myself; I had long had an inkling of it. Now the

whole of idealist philosophy stood before me in modified form. What's a sleepless night compared to that!"
Rudolf Steiner begins communicating with leading thinkers of the day, who send him books in return, which he reads eagerly.

July: "I am not one of those who dives into the day like an animal in human form. I pursue a quite specific goal, an idealistic aim—knowledge of the truth! This cannot be done offhandedly. It requires the greatest striving in the world, free of all egotism, and equally of all resignation."

August: Steiner puts down on paper for the first time thoughts for a "Philosophy of Freedom." "The striving for the absolute: this human yearning is freedom." He also seeks to outline a "peasant philosophy," describing what the worldview of a "peasant"—one who lives close to the earth and the old ways—really is.

1881–1882: Felix Koguzki, the herb gatherer, reveals himself to be the envoy of another, higher initiatory personality, who instructs Rudolf Steiner to penetrate Fichte's philosophy and to master modern scientific thinking as a preparation for right entry into the spirit. This "Master" also teaches him the double (evolutionary and involutionary) nature of time.

1882: Through the offices of Karl Julius Schröer, Rudolf Steiner is asked by Joseph Kurschner to edit Goethe's scientific writings for the *Deutschen National-Literatur* edition. He writes "A Possible Critique of Atomistic Concepts" and sends it to Friedrich Theodor Vischer.

1883: Rudolf Steiner completes his college studies and begins work on the Goethe project.

1884: First volume of Goethe's *Scientific Writings* (CW 1) appears (March). He lectures on Goethe and Lessing, and Goethe's approach to science. In July, he enters the household of Ladislaus and Pauline Specht as tutor to the four Specht boys. He will live there until 1890. At this time, he meets Josef Breuer (1842–1925), the coauthor with Sigmund Freud of *Studies in Hysteria*, who is the Specht family doctor.

1885: While continuing to edit Goethe's writings, Rudolf Steiner reads deeply in contemporary philosophy (Edouard von Hartmann, Johannes Volkelt, and Richard Wahle, among others).

1886: May: Rudolf Steiner sends Kurschner the manuscript of *Outlines of Goethe's Theory of Knowledge* (CW 2), which appears in October, and which he sends out widely. He also meets the poet Marie Eugenie Delle Grazie and writes "Nature and Our Ideals" for her. He attends her salon, where he meets many priests, theologians, and philosophers, who will become his friends. Meanwhile, the director of the Goethe Archive in Weimar requests his collaboration with the *Sophien* edition of Goethe's works, particularly the writings on color.

1887: At the beginning of the year, Rudolf Steiner is very sick. As the year progresses and his health improves, he becomes increasingly "a man of letters," lecturing, writing essays, and taking part in Austrian cultural life. In August–September, the second volume of Goethe's *Scientific Writings* appears.

1888: January–July: Rudolf Steiner assumes editorship of the "German Weekly" (*Deutsche Wochenschrift*). He begins lecturing more intensively, giving, for example, a lecture titled "Goethe as Father of a New Aesthetics." He meets and becomes soul friends with Friedrich Eckstein (1861–1939), a vegetarian, philosopher of symbolism, alchemist, and musician, who will introduce him to various spiritual currents (including Theosophy) and with whom he will meditate and interpret esoteric and alchemical texts.

1889: Rudolf Steiner first reads Nietzsche (*Beyond Good and Evil*). He encounters Theosophy again and learns of Madame Blavatsky in the Theosophical circle around Marie Lang (1858–1934). Here he also meets well-known figures of Austrian life, as well as esoteric figures like the occultist Franz Hartman and Karl Leinigen-Billigen (translator of C.G. Harrison's *The Transcendental Universe*). During this period, Steiner first reads A.P. Sinnett's *Esoteric Buddhism* and Mabel Collins's *Light on the Path*. He also begins traveling, visiting Budapest, Weimar, and Berlin (where he meets philosopher Edouard von Hartman).

1890: Rudolf Steiner finishes volume 3 of Goethe's scientific writings. He begins his doctoral dissertation, which will become *Truth and Science* (CW 3). He also meets the poet and feminist Rosa Mayreder (1858–1938), with whom he can exchange his most intimate thoughts. In September, Rudolf Steiner moves to Weimar to work in the Goethe-Schiller Archive.

1891: Volume 3 of the Kurschner edition of Goethe appears. Meanwhile, Rudolf Steiner edits Goethe's studies in mineralogy and scientific writings for the *Sophien* edition. He meets Ludwig Laistner of the Cotta Publishing Company, who asks for a book on the basic question of metaphysics. From this will result, ultimately, *The Philosophy of Freedom* (CW 4), which will be published not by Cotta but by Emil Felber. In October, Rudolf Steiner takes the oral exam for a doctorate in philosophy, mathematics, and mechanics at Rostock University, receiving his doctorate on the twenty-sixth. In November, he gives his first lecture on Goethe's "Fairy Tale" in Vienna.

1892: Rudolf Steiner continues work at the Goethe-Schiller Archive and on his *Philosophy of Freedom*. *Truth and Science*, his doctoral dissertation, is published. Steiner undertakes to write introductions to books on Schopenhauer and Jean Paul for Cotta. At year's end, he finds lodging with Anna Eunike, née Schulz (1853–1911), a widow with four daughters and a son. He also develops a friendship with Otto Erich Hartleben (1864–1905) with whom he shares literary interests.

1893: Rudolf Steiner begins his habit of producing many reviews and articles. In March, he gives a lecture titled "Hypnotism, with Reference to Spiritism." In September, volume 4 of the Kurschner edition is completed. In November, *The Philosophy of Freedom* appears. This year, too, he meets John Henry Mackay (1864–1933), the anarchist, and Max Stirner, a scholar and biographer.

1894: Rudolf Steiner meets Elisabeth Förster Nietzsche, the philosopher's sister, and begins to read Nietzsche in earnest, beginning with the as yet unpublished *Antichrist*. He also meets Ernst Haeckel (1834–1919). In the fall, he begins to write *Nietzsche, A Fighter against His Time* (CW 5).

1895: May: *Nietzsche, A Fighter against His Time* appears.

1896: January 22: Rudolf Steiner sees Friedrich Nietzsche for the first and only time. Moves between the Nietzsche and the Goethe-Schiller Archives, where he completes his work before year's end. He falls out with Elisabeth Förster Nietzsche, thus ending his association with the Nietzsche Archive.

1897: Rudolf Steiner finishes the manuscript of *Goethe's Worldview* (CW 6). He moves to Berlin with Anna Eunike and begins editorship of the *Magazin fur Literatur*. From now on, Steiner will write countless reviews, literary and philosophical articles, and so on. He begins lecturing at the "Free Literary Society." In September, he attends the Zionist Congress in Basel. He sides with Dreyfus in the Dreyfus affair.

1898: Rudolf Steiner is very active as an editor in the political, artistic, and theatrical life of Berlin. He becomes friendly with John Henry Mackay and poet Ludwig Jacobowski (1868–1900). He joins Jacobowski's circle of writers, artists, and scientists—"The Coming Ones" (*Die Kommenden*)—and contributes lectures to the group until 1903. He also lectures at the "League for College Pedagogy." He writes an article for Goethe's sesquicentennial, "Goethe's Secret Revelation," on the "Fairy Tale of the Green Snake and the Beautiful Lily."

1898–99: "This was a trying time for my soul as I looked at Christianity. . . . I was able to progress only by contemplating, by means of spiritual perception, the evolution of Christianity. . . . Conscious knowledge of real Christianity began to dawn in me around the turn of the century. This seed continued to develop. My soul trial occurred shortly before the beginning of the twentieth century. It was decisive for my soul's development that I stood spiritually before the Mystery of Golgotha in a deep and solemn celebration of knowledge."

1899: Rudolf Steiner begins teaching and giving lectures and lecture cycles at the Workers' College, founded by Wilhelm Liebknecht (1826–1900). He will continue to do so until 1904. Writes: *Literature and Spiritual Life in the Nineteenth Century; Individualism in Philosophy; Haeckel and His Opponents; Poetry in the Present;* and begins what will become (fifteen years later) *The Riddles of Philosophy* (CW 18). He also meets many artists and writers, including Käthe Kollwitz, Stefan Zweig, and Rainer Maria Rilke. On October 31, he marries Anna Eunike.

1900: "I thought that the turn of the century must bring humanity a new light. It seemed to me that the separation of human thinking and willing from the spirit had peaked. A turn or reversal of direction in human evolution seemed to me a necessity." Rudolf Steiner finishes *World and Life Views in the Nineteenth Century* (the second part of what will become *The Riddles of Philosophy*) and dedicates it to Ernst Haeckel.

It is published in March. He continues lecturing at *Die Kommenden*, whose leadership he assumes after the death of Jacobowski. Also, he gives the Gutenberg Jubilee lecture before 7,000 typesetters and printers. In September, Rudolf Steiner is invited by Count and Countess Brockdorff to lecture in the Theosophical Library. His first lecture is on Nietzsche. His second lecture is titled "Goethe's Secret Revelation." October 6, he begins a lecture cycle on the mystics that will become *Mystics after Modernism* (CW 7). November–December: "Marie von Sivers appears in the audience...." Also in November, Steiner gives his first lecture at the Giordano Bruno Bund (where he will continue to lecture until May, 1905). He speaks on Bruno and modern Rome, focusing on the importance of the philosophy of Thomas Aquinas as monism.

1901: In continual financial straits, Rudolf Steiner's early friends Moritz Zitter and Rosa Mayreder help support him. In October, he begins the lecture cycle *Christianity as Mystical Fact* (CW 8) at the Theosophical Library. In November, he gives his first "Theosophical lecture" on Goethe's "Fairy Tale" in Hamburg at the invitation of Wilhelm Hubbe-Schleiden. He also attends a tea to celebrate the founding of the Theosophical Society at Count and Countess Brockdorff's. He gives a lecture cycle, "From Buddha to Christ," for the circle of the *Kommenden*. November 17, Marie von Sivers asks Rudolf Steiner if Theosophy does not need a Western-Christian spiritual movement (to complement Theosophy's Eastern emphasis). "The question was posed. Now, following spiritual laws, I could begin to give an answer...." In December, Rudolf Steiner writes his first article for a Theosophical publication. At year's end, the Brockdorffs and possibly Wilhelm Hubbe-Schleiden ask Rudolf Steiner to join the Theosophical Society and undertake the leadership of the German section. Rudolf Steiner agrees, on the condition that Marie von Sivers (then in Italy) work with him.

1902: Beginning in January, Rudolf Steiner attends the opening of the Workers' School in Spandau with Rosa Luxemberg (1870–1919). January 17, Rudolf Steiner joins the Theosophical Society. In April, he is asked to become general secretary of the German Section of the Theosophical Society, and works on preparations for its founding. In July, he visits London for a Theosophical congress. He meets Bertram Keightly, G.R.S. Mead, A.P. Sinnett, and Annie Besant, among others. In September, *Christianity as Mystical Fact* appears. In October, Rudolf Steiner gives his first public lecture on Theosophy ("Monism and Theosophy") to about three hundred people at the Giordano Bruno Bund. From October 19–21, the German Section of the Theosophical Society has its first meeting; Rudolf Steiner is the general secretary, and Annie Besant attends. Steiner lectures on practical karma studies. On October 23, Annie Besant inducts Rudolf Steiner into the Esoteric School of the Theosophical Society. On October 25, Steiner begins a weekly series of lectures: "The Field of Theosophy." During this year, Rudolf Steiner also first meets Ita Wegman (1876–1943), who will become his close collaborator in his final years.

1903: Rudolf Steiner holds about 300 lectures and seminars. In May, the first issue of the periodical *Luzifer* appears. In June, Rudolf Steiner visits London for the first meeting of the Federation of the European Sections of the Theosophical Society, where he meets Colonel Olcott. He begins to write *Theosophy* (CW 9).

1904: Rudolf Steiner continues lecturing at the Workers' College and elsewhere (about 90 lectures), while lecturing intensively all over Germany among Theosophists (about 140 lectures). In February, he meets Carl Unger (1878–1929), who will become a member of the board of the Anthroposophical Society (1913). In March, he meets Michael Bauer (1871–1929), a Christian mystic, who will also be on the board. In May, *Theosophy* appears, with the dedication: "To the spirit of Giordano Bruno." Rudolf Steiner and Marie von Sivers visit London for meetings with Annie Besant. In June, Rudolf Steiner and Marie von Sivers attend the meeting of the Federation of European Sections of the Theosophical Society in Amsterdam. In July, Steiner begins the articles in *Lucifer-Gnosis* that will become *How to Know Higher Worlds* (CW 10) and *Cosmic Memory* (CW 11). In September, Annie Besant visits Germany. In December, Steiner lectures on Freemasonry. He mentions the High Grade Masonry derived from John Yarker and represented by Theodore Reuss and Karl Kellner as a blank slate "into which a good image could be placed."

1905: This year, Steiner ends his non-Theosophical lecturing activity. Supported by Marie von Sivers, his Theosophical lecturing—both in public and in the Theosophical Society—increases significantly: "The German Theosophical Movement is of exceptional importance." Steiner recommends reading, among others, Fichte, Jacob Boehme, and Angelus Silesius. He begins to introduce Christian themes into Theosophy. He also begins to work with doctors (Felix Peipers and Ludwig Noll). In July, he is in London for the Federation of European Sections, where he attends a lecture by Annie Besant: "I have seldom seen Mrs. Besant speak in so inward and heartfelt a manner...." "Through Mrs. Besant I have found the way to H. P. Blavatsky." September to October, he gives a course of thirty-one lectures for a small group of esoteric students. In October, the annual meeting of the German Section of the Theosophical Society, which still remains very small, takes place. Rudolf Steiner reports membership has risen from 121 to 377 members. In November, seeking to establish esoteric "continuity," Rudolf Steiner and Marie von Sivers participate in a "Memphis-Misraim" Masonic ceremony. They pay forty-five marks for membership. "Yesterday, you saw how little remains of former esoteric institutions." "We are dealing only with a 'framework'... for the present, nothing lies behind it. The occult powers have completely withdrawn."

1906: Expansion of Theosophical work. Rudolf Steiner gives about 245 lectures, only 44 of which take place in Berlin. Cycles are given in Paris, Leipzig, Stuttgart, and Munich. Esoteric work also intensifies. Rudolf Steiner begins writing *An Outline of Esoteric Science* (CW 13). In January, Rudolf Steiner receives permission (a patent) from the Great Orient of the Scottish A & A Thirty-Three Degree Rite of the Order of the Ancient Freemasons of the Memphis-Misraim Rite to direct a chapter under the name "Mystica Aeterna." This will become the "Cognitive Cultic Section" (also called "Misraim Service") of the Esoteric School. (See: *From the History and Contents of the Cognitive Cultic Section* [CW 264].) During this time, Steiner also meets Albert Schweitzer. In May, he is in Paris, where he visits Edouard Schuré. Many Russians attend his lectures (including Konstantin Balmont, Dimitri Mereszkovski, Zinaida Hippius, and Maximilian Woloshin). He attends the General Meeting of the European Federation of the Theosophical Society, at which Col. Olcott is present for the last time. He spends the year's end in Venice and Rome, where he writes and works on his translation of H. P. Blavatsky's *Key to Theosophy*.

1907: Further expansion of the German Theosophical Movement according to the Rosicrucian directive to "introduce spirit into the world"—in education, in social questions, in art, and in science. In February, Col. Olcott dies in Adyar. Before he dies, Olcott indicates that "the Masters" wish Annie Besant to succeed him: much politicking ensues. Rudolf Steiner supports Besant's candidacy. April–May: preparations for the Congress of the Federation of European Sections of the Theosophical Society—the great, watershed Whitsun "Munich Congress," attended by Annie Besant and others. Steiner decides to separate Eastern and Western (Christian-Rosicrucian) esoteric schools. He takes his esoteric school out of the Theosophical Society (Besant and Rudolf Steiner are "in harmony" on this). Steiner makes his first lecture tours to Austria and Hungary. That summer, he is in Italy. In September, he visits Edouard Schuré, who will write the introduction to the French edition of *Christianity as Mystical Fact* in Barr, Alsace. Rudolf Steiner writes the autobiographical statement known as the "Barr Document." In *Luzifer–Gnosis*, "The Education of the Child" appears.

1908: The movement grows (membership: 1150). Lecturing expands. Steiner makes his first extended lecture tour to Holland and Scandinavia, as well as visits to Naples and Sicily. Themes: St. John's Gospel, the Apocalypse, Egypt, science, philosophy, and logic. *Lucifer-Gnosis* ceases publication. In Berlin, Marie von Sivers (with Johanna Mücke [1864–1949]) forms the *Philosophisch-Theosophisch* (after 1915 *Philosophisch-Anthroposophisch*) *Verlag* to publish Steiner's work. Steiner gives lecture cycles titled *The Gospel of St. John* (CW 103) and *The Apocalypse* (104).

1909: *An Outline of Esoteric Science* appears. Lecturing and travel continue. Rudolf Steiner's spiritual research expands to include the polarity of Lucifer and Ahriman; the work of great individualities in history; the

Maitreya Buddha and the Bodhisattvas; spiritual economy (CW 109); the work of the spiritual hierarchies in heaven and on Earth (CW 110). He also deepens and intensifies his research into the Gospels, giving lectures on the Gospel of St. Luke (CW 114) with the first mention of two Jesus children. Meets and becomes friends with Christian Morgenstern (1871–1914). In April, he lays the foundation stone for the Malsch model—the building that will lead to the first Goetheanum. In May, the International Congress of the Federation of European Sections of the Theosophical Society takes place in Budapest. Rudolf Steiner receives the Subba Row medal for *How to Know Higher Worlds*. During this time, Charles W. Leadbeater discovers Jiddu Krishnamurti (1895–1986) and proclaims him the future "world teacher," the bearer of the Maitreya Buddha and the "reappearing Christ." In October, Steiner delivers seminal lectures on "anthroposophy," which he will try, unsuccessfully, to rework over the next years into the unfinished work, *Anthroposophy (A Fragment)* (CW 45).

1910: New themes: *The Reappearance of Christ in the Etheric* (CW 118); *The Fifth Gospel* (CW 148); *The Mission of Folk Souls* (CW 121); *Occult History* (CW 126); the evolving development of etheric cognitive capacities. Rudolf Steiner continues his Gospel research with *The Gospel of St. Matthew* (CW 123). In January, his father dies. In April, he takes a month-long trip to Italy, including Rome, Monte Cassino, and Sicily. He also visits Scandinavia again. July–August, he writes the first mystery drama, *The Portal of Initiation* (CW 14). In November, he gives "psychosophy" lectures. In December, he submits "On the Psychological Foundations and Epistemological Framework of Theosophy" to the International Philosophical Congress in Bologna.

1911: The crisis in the Theosophical Society deepens. In January, "The Order of the Rising Sun," which will soon become "The Order of the Star in the East," is founded for the coming world teacher, Krishnamurti. At the same time, Marie von Sivers, Rudolf Steiner's coworker, falls ill. Fewer lectures are given, but important new ground is broken. In Prague, in March, Steiner meets Franz Kafka (1883–1924) and Hugo Bergmann (1883–1975). In April, he delivers his paper to the Philosophical Congress. He writes the second mystery drama, *The Soul's Probation* (CW 14). Also, while Marie von Sivers is convalescing, Rudolf Steiner begins work on *Calendar 1912/1913*, which will contain the "Calendar of the Soul" meditations. On March 19, Anna (Eunike) Steiner dies. In September, Rudolf Steiner visits Einsiedeln, birthplace of Paracelsus. In December, Friedrich Rittelmeyer, future founder of the Christian Community, meets Rudolf Steiner. The *Johannes-Bauverein*, the "building committee," which would lead to the first Goetheanum (first planned for Munich), is also founded, and a preliminary committee for the founding of an independent association is created that, in the following year, will become the Anthroposophical Society. Important lecture cycles include *Occult Physiology* (CW 128);

Wonders of the World (CW 129); *From Jesus to Christ* (CW 131). Other themes: esoteric Christianity; Christian Rosenkreutz; the spiritual guidance of humanity; the sense world and the world of the spirit.

1912: Despite the ongoing, now increasing crisis in the Theosophical Society, much is accomplished: *Calendar 1912/1913* is published; eurythmy is created; both the third mystery drama, *The Guardian of the Threshold* (CW 14) and *A Way of Self-Knowledge* (CW 16) are written. New (or renewed) themes include life between death and rebirth and karma and reincarnation. Other lecture cycles: *Spiritual Beings in the Heavenly Bodies and the Kingdoms of Nature* (CW 136); *The Human Being in the Light of Occultism, Theosophy, and Philosophy* (CW 137); *The Gospel of St. Mark* (CW 139); and *The Bhagavad Gita and the Epistles of Paul* (CW 142). On May 8, Rudolf Steiner celebrates White Lotus Day, H.P. Blavatsky's death day, which he had faithfully observed for the past decade, for the last time. In August, Rudolf Steiner suggests the "independent association" be called the "Anthroposophical Society." In September, the first eurythmy course takes place. Also, with Marie von Sivers, he first visits Dornach, near Basel, Switzerland, and they stand on the hill where the Goetheanum will be. In November, a Theosophical Society lodge is opened by direct mandate from Adyar (Annie Besant). In December, a meeting of the German section occurs at which it is decided that belonging to the Order of the Star of the East is incompatible with membership in the Theosophical Society. December 28: informal founding of the Anthroposophical Society in Berlin.

1913: Expulsion of the German section from the Theosophical Society. February 2–3: Foundation meeting of the Anthroposophical Society. Board members include: Marie von Sivers, Michael Bauer, and Carl Unger. September 20: Laying of the foundation stone for the *Johannes Bau* (Goetheanum) in Dornach. Building begins immediately. The third mystery drama, *The Soul's Awakening* (CW 14), is completed. Also: *The Threshold of the Spiritual World* (CW 147). Lecture cycles include: *The Bhagavad Gita and the Epistles of Paul* and *The Esoteric Meaning of the Bhagavad Gita* (CW 146), which the Russian philosopher Nikolai Berdyaev attends; *The Mysteries of the East and of Christianity* (CW 144); *The Effects of Esoteric Development* (CW 145); and *The Fifth Gospel* (CW 148). In May, Rudolf Steiner is in London and Paris, where anthroposophical work continues.

1914: Building continues on the *Johannes Bau* (Goetheanum) in Dornach, with artists and coworkers from seventeen nations. The general assembly of the Anthroposophical Society takes place. In May, Rudolf Steiner visits Paris, as well as Chartres Cathedral. June 28: assassination in Sarajevo ("Now the catastrophe has happened!"). August 1: War is declared. Rudolf Steiner returns to Germany from Dornach—he will travel back and forth. He writes the last chapter of *The Riddles of Philosophy*. Lecture cycles include: *Human and Cosmic Thought* (CW 151); *Inner Being of*

Humanity between Death and a New Birth (CW 153); *Occult Reading and Occult Hearing* (CW 156). December 24: marriage of Rudolf Steiner and Marie von Sivers.

1915: Building continues. Life after death becomes a major theme, also art. Writes: *Thoughts during a Time of War* (CW 24). Lectures include: *The Secret of Death* (CW 159); *The Uniting of Humanity through the Christ Impulse* (CW 165).

1916: Rudolf Steiner begins work with Edith Maryon (1872–1924) on the sculpture "The Representative of Humanity" ("The Group"—Christ, Lucifer, and Ahriman). He also works with the alchemist Alexander von Bernus on the quarterly *Das Reich*. He writes *The Riddle of Humanity* (CW 20). Lectures include: *Necessity and Freedom in World History and Human Action* (CW 166); *Past and Present in the Human Spirit* (CW 167); *The Karma of Vocation* (CW 172); *The Karma of Untruthfulness* (CW 173).

1917: Russian Revolution. The U.S. enters the war. Building continues. Rudolf Steiner delineates the idea of the "threefold nature of the human being" (in a public lecture March 15) and the "threefold nature of the social organism" (hammered out in May–June with the help of Otto von Lerchenfeld and Ludwig Polzer-Hoditz in the form of two documents titled *Memoranda*, which were distributed in high places). August–September: Rudolf Steiner writes *The Riddles of the Soul* (CW 20). Also: commentary on "The Chemical Wedding of Christian Rosenkreutz" for Alexander Bernus (*Das Reich*). Lectures include: *The Karma of Materialism* (CW 176); *The Spiritual Background of the Outer World: The Fall of the Spirits of Darkness* (CW 177).

1918: March 18: peace treaty of Brest-Litovsk—"Now everything will truly enter chaos! What is needed is cultural renewal." June: Rudolf Steiner visits Karlstein (Grail) Castle outside Prague. Lecture cycle: *From Symptom to Reality in Modern History* (CW 185). In mid-November, Emil Molt, of the Waldorf-Astoria Cigarette Company, has the idea of founding a school for his workers' children.

1919: Focus on the threefold social organism: tireless travel, countless lectures, meetings, and publications. At the same time, a new public stage of Anthroposophy emerges as cultural renewal begins. The coming years will see initiatives in pedagogy, medicine, pharmacology, and agriculture. January 27: threefold meeting: " We must first of all, with the money we have, found free schools that can bring people what they need." February: first public eurythmy performance in Zurich. Also: "Appeal to the German People" (CW 24), circulated March 6 as a newspaper insert. In April, *Toward Social Renewal* (CW 23)—"perhaps the most widely read of all books on politics appearing since the war"—appears. Rudolf Steiner is asked to undertake the "direction and leadership" of the school founded by the Waldorf-Astoria Company. Rudolf Steiner begins to talk about the "renewal" of education. May 30: a building is selected and purchased for the future Waldorf School.

August–September: Rudolf Steiner gives a lecture course for Waldorf teachers, *The Foundations of Human Experience (Study of Man)* (CW 293). September 7: Opening of the first Waldorf School. December (into January): first science course, the *Light Course* (CW 320).

1920: The Waldorf School flourishes. New threefold initiatives. Founding of limited companies *Der Kommenden Tag* and *Futurum A.G.* to infuse spiritual values into the economic realm. Rudolf Steiner also focuses on the sciences. Lectures: *Introducing Anthroposophical Medicine* (CW 312); *The Warmth Course* (CW 321); *The Boundaries of Natural Science* (CW 322); *The Redemption of Thinking* (CW 74). February: Johannes Werner Klein—later a cofounder of the Christian Community—asks Rudolf Steiner about the possibility of a "religious renewal," a "Johannine church." In March, Rudolf Steiner gives the first course for doctors and medical students. In April, a divinity student asks Rudolf Steiner a second time about the possibility of religious renewal. September 27–October 16: anthroposophical "college course." December: lectures titled *The Search for the New Isis* (CW 202).

1921: Rudolf Steiner continues his intensive work on cultural renewal, including the uphill battle for the threefold social order. "College" arts, scientific, theological, and medical courses include: *The Astronomy Course* (CW 323); *Observation, Mathematics, and Scientific Experiment* (CW 324); the *Second Medical Course* (CW 313); *Color* (CW 291). In June and September–October, Rudolf Steiner also gives the first two "priests' courses" (CW 342 and 343). The "youth movement" gains momentum. Magazines are founded: *Die Drei* (January), and—under the editorship of Albert Steffen (1884–1963)—the weekly, *Das Goetheanum* (August). In February–March, Rudolf Steiner takes his first trip outside Germany since the war (Holland). On April 7, Steiner receives a letter regarding "religious renewal," and May 22–23, he agrees to address the question in a practical way. In June, the Clinical-Therapeutic Institute opens in Arlesheim under the direction of Dr. Ita Wegman. In August, the Chemical-Pharmaceutical Laboratory opens in Arlesheim (Oskar Schmiedel and Ita Wegman, directors). The Clinical-Therapeutic Institute is inaugurated in Stuttgart (Dr. Ludwig Noll, director); also the Research Laboratory in Dornach (Ehrenfried Pfeiffer and Gunther Wachsmuth, directors). In November–December, Rudolf Steiner visits Norway.

1922: The first half of the year involves very active public lecturing (thousands attend); in the second half, Rudolf Steiner begins to withdraw and turn toward the Society—"The Society is asleep." It is "too weak" to do what is asked of it. The businesses—*Die Kommenden Tag* and *Futura A.G.*—fail. In January, with the help of an agent, Steiner undertakes a twelve-city German tour, accompanied by eurythmy performances. In two weeks he speaks to more than 2,000 people. In April, he gives a "college course" in The Hague. He also visits England. In June, he is in Vienna for the East-West Congress. In August–September, he is back in England for the Oxford Conference on Education. Returning to Dornach, he gives the lectures *Philosophy, Cosmology, and Religion* (CW 215), and gives the third priest's course (CW 344). On September 16, The Christian Community is founded. In October–November, Steiner is in Holland and England. He also speaks to the youth: *The Youth Course* (CW 217). In December, Steiner gives lectures titled *The Origins of Natural Science* (CW 326), and *Humanity and the World of Stars: The Spiritual Communion of Humanity* (CW 219). December 31: Fire at the Goetheanum, which is destroyed.

1923: Despite the fire, Rudolf Steiner continues his work unabated. A very hard year. Internal dispersion, dissension, and apathy abound. There is conflict—between old and new visions—within the society. A wake-up call is needed, and Rudolf Steiner responds with renewed lecturing vitality. His focus: the spiritual context of human life; initiation science; the course of the year; and community building. As a foundation for an artistic school, he creates a series of pastel sketches. Lecture cycles: *The Anthroposophic Movement* (CW 258); *Initiation Science* (CW 227) (in England at the Penmaenmawr Summer School); *The Four Seasons and the Archangels* (CW 229); *Harmony of the Creative Word* (CW 230); *The Supersensible Human* (CW 231), given in Holland for the founding of the Dutch society. On November 10, in response to the failed Hitler-Ludendorf putsch in Munich, Steiner closes his Berlin residence and moves the *Philosophisch-Anthroposophisch Verlag* (Press) to Dornach. On December 9, Steiner begins the serialization of his *Autobiography: The Course of My Life* (CW 28) in *Das Goetheanum*. It will continue to appear weekly, without a break, until his death. Late December-early January: Rudolf Steiner refounds the Anthroposophical Society (about 12,000 members internationally) and takes over its leadership. The new board members are: Marie Steiner, Ita Wegman, Albert Steffen, Elizabeth Vreede, and Guenther Wachsmuth. (See *The Christmas Meeting for the Founding of the General Anthroposophical Society* [CW 260]. Accompanying lectures: *Mystery Knowledge and Mystery Centers* [CW 232]; *World History in the Light of Anthroposophy* [CW 233].) December 25: the Foundation Stone is laid (in the hearts of members) in the form of the "Foundation Stone Meditation."

1924: January 1: having founded the Anthroposophical Society and taken over its leadership, Rudolf Steiner has the task of "reforming" it. The process begins with a weekly newssheet ("What's Happening in the Anthroposophical Society") in which Rudolf Steiner's "Letters to Members" and "Anthroposophical Leading Thoughts" appear (CW 26). The next step is the creation of a new esoteric class, the "first class" of the "School for Spiritual Science" (which was to have been followed, had Rudolf Steiner lived longer, by two more advanced classes). Then comes a new language for anthroposophy—practical, phenomenological, and direct—and Rudolf Steiner creates the model for the second Goetheanum. He begins the series of extensive "karma lectures" (CW 235–40); and finally, responding to needs, he creates two new initiatives: biodynamic agriculture and curative education. After the middle of the year, rumors begin to circulate regarding Steiner's health. Lectures: January–February, *Anthroposophy* (CW 234); February: *Eurythmy as Visible Singing* (CW 278); June: *The Agriculture Course* (CW 327); June–July: *Eurythmy as Visible Speech* (CW 279); *Curative Education* (CW 317); August: (England, "Second International Summer School") *Initiation Consciousness: True and False Paths in Spiritual Investigation* (CW 243); September: *Pastoral Medicine* (CW 318). On September 26, for the first time, Rudolf Steiner cancels a lecture. On September 28, he gives his last lecture. On September 29, he withdraws to his studio in the carpenter's shop; now he is definitively ill. Cared for by Ita Wegman, he continues working, however, and writing the weekly installments of his *Autobiography* and *Letters to the Members/Leading Thoughts* (CW 26).

1925: Rudolf Steiner, while continuing to work, continues to weaken. He finishes *Extending Practical Medicine* (CW 27) with Ita Wegman.

On March 30, around ten in the morning, Rudolf Steiner dies.

INDEX

T

U

V

W

Z